# future flowers, whispered war-cries

## poetic truth of a Kingdom

### hosanna emily

*i always wonder how ordinary moments can be praise*
*like how the simplest brush smeared with paint makes*
*something beautiful.*
*or like if a copyright page could be a poem.*
*ahh, praise, for the One i love.*
*in the title:*

future flowers, whispered war-cries: *poetic truth of a Kingdom*

*and more,*

Heart Like His Publishing
ISBN: 978-1-969314-02-5

*for worship was in the cover design:*

Cover illustration © Praise Evangeline
Cover design © Josiah Chad

*and in the messy, in-betweens of the pages:*

printing done in the United States of America
second edition published 2025

*praise in His words which are sweet like honey, fresh like water*
*and a treasure i live for:*

*let all be praise,*
*even copyright words smeared on a page,*
*to our King who is worthy.*

## roots

## thorns

## *blossoms*

## *behind the poems*

*"The Kingdom of Heaven is like a treasure hidden in a field, which a man found and rehid. Then out of his joy he goes and sells everything he has and buys that field."*

Matthew 13:44

*author testimony*

hi friend.

before this book gets all poetic-y and we dive together into beautiful words of story and meaning, this book starts with a testimony:

a testimony is when a soul steps up, grabs a mic, and declares evidence of a Truth,

and this girl wants to testify of Jesus.

these poems are only here because of Him. i remember a day when it felt like the enemy squelched these words and threw them across the sea to drown—like how my laptop felt when my water bottle spilled onto it. i remember that sinking-in feeling that the words were just gone. they were part of me disappeared in a moment. the laptop was dead.

but God.

those words have changed my life.

this "but God" moment might not seem miraculous, but when, months later, God revealed a way to recover the lost files and those old poems appeared alive again, part of me was reborn. this book wouldn't be here without that tiny moment of near tears and praise, and i testify that God has purpose in this book.

He has done "but God" moments again and again, bringing this broken, sinful girl of a person to a place of complete forgiveness and restoration where i just dance for joy as His princess, and that's why i'm a hopelessly-in-love follower.

there's two "but God" moments this book seeks to testify of:

the first, the Day God's love for us selfish, hopeless people was so great that He left His matchless throne to become a humble, suffering servant—Jesus—to receive the punishment of death we rightfully deserved. He suffered for every wrong we committed. He made a way for us to be forgiven and restored, and, conquering death, He rose and is on His heavenly throne.

and the second Day when that God will come again as a conquering King to judge His people, to punish all evil and to save those who are purified by the first Day and reward their works. He will establish His Kingdom, and it's going to be incredible.

that's my testimony.

it's changed my life. it's why i write poetry. there's so many testimonies behind in this book and even how He provided the poems when they should have drowned.

but His testimony of those Days are what changes everything.

i challenge you to pursue your own "but God" story.

# dedication

**dear Warrior Poet,**

this book is for you:

for the poet in you who was made to create beauty in whatever form God put before you and bring Him glory in and through that beauty.

maybe you're a poet in words, sweeping your pen across paper to spread His Gospel of good news to hearts beyond your hands.

but this is also for the woman who makes poetry through the hearts of her children, cleaning and cooking again to serve her King.

for the child who makes poetry by simply loving the people God puts around them and doing her chores, her school, and every little act of love well for the Lord.

for the man with eyes for the lost as he is found faithfully furthering the Kingdom in whatever facet of life God sets before him.

for every person who seeks to fulfill their calling of spreading His Kingdom wherever they are with a God who loves them passionately because they know He is drawing them to that coming

Kingdom where they can be with Him in ultimate joy, as a Father joying in the presence of His children.

ahh, you Warrior Poet, this book is for you.

you'll find it in these sectioned themes:

blossoms—*love*, to spur you on to know Jesus intimately, to have a love relationship with Him which results in obedience to His words which are precious

thorns—*hope*, to understand the future God has for us which makes ordinary days become something incredibly purposeful and helps us see beyond the darkness

roots—*faith*, the action of believing because of the love and hope, the determination to be found faithful, the continuance despite whatever this world throws at you

it is my humble prayer that these poems of faith, hope, and love are a beckoning call to dive deeper into a relationship with the God who created you and seek first His Kingdom.

and if you're not yet a warrior poet, i beg you to join this army. it's the most glorious, upward calling of fulfillment that you can imagine.

shalom oasis,
*hosanna emily*

a word, a life

i want to write something beautiful
like the rain that drips on my paper.

roses stained pink—
kissed by freezing dew drops,
or sunflowers bowed down—
reaching for sticky soil
because their beauty is just too great,
too heavy for their emerald trunks.
they're Hope, dead seeds a picture of something glorious
to come,
wilted fuchsia petals dripping pink like ink to last forever.

yes, i want to write like the flowers
something almost too lovely for the world's eyes.
they forget, and we need to remind them

that Faith is believing to look
past deadness of wilting sunflowers to seeds within,
knowing God's promises are true,
and, like the rain, letting go.

fall free
to embrace the roses,
drip on sunflowers,
splash onto thirsty ground,
and truly live.
i call it Love—the action of living in that beauty.

i lift my chin to the rain and see it clear
crystal in those three:
in Faith and Hope and Love.

i want to write something beautiful
because i want to live
embracing Beauty.

*roots*

faith in something we cannot yet see

Caroline Rutledge

# abundance

on bushes with limbs hanging low
weighted by a harvest to come,
sweetness of berries hidden
for the touch, the taste.

on the heart of a wordsmith
where stories flow faster than the ink of a pen,
the joy! the dreams!
mixed with the callouses of fingers
and the tears of a creator,
or the nights he lies awake.

in the eyes of the broken,
a different harvest, unseen
of so many souls.

but perhaps it means a change.
because fruit doesn't gather itself
nor is a book self-written.
but it takes hands
and hearts and time and faithfulness
to testify, to love.
if it wins souls,
shall we?

ah, Father, for this gift of overflowing,
arms wide, You drench us.
may we do all that: harvest, create, and testify.
may abundance create a river
we traverse with You
and be found faithful,
faithfully gathering.

Tarissa Hughes

# a glimpse

awakening to crystal gems of frost
icy rainbows, morning sun
colors beyond, in words we have lost
and i wonder if i see
a glimpse of the New Earth.

the hot, red clay of Georgia earth
turfs of grass with golden heads
and every street, hundred souls of worth.

white fields like snow yet where cotton grows
each set of eyes, longing hope
beyond pretty words or sun that glows
and i wonder if i see
a glimpse of the New Earth.

a glimpse, a glimpse, forever true

a King, a Kingdom, returning new.

# blind color

there was a time when i couldn't see

colors

even though

i thought i could.

as if my eyes were closed

although open,

or if it was night

even in day.

i saw colors—or their apparitions,

the ghosts of color,

over and over, every

day.

but green was grey

and blue, white

like an old-fashioned world in film,

and i didn't know the difference

until that Voice:

it whispered: *red.* i saw it.

among the old, dead leaves

one crimson sprig, like blood pulsing.

it was color.

and it was beauty.

that Voice. *blue*

I looked up into never ending expanse

deeper than oceans yet close

enough to touch.

the Voice. *yellow* and *green,*

*pink* and a million others.

i saw rainbows and flowers and

works of art

in every leaf

   every raindrop

   every face

      beauty.

the Voice kept on, things beyond this world

like song. smell. touch. love.

and i wonder if all this is Life.

               Real Life.

and if anyone else can see colors or

if they just think

they can.

## collage called the Church

a million slivers of wood pasted together

browns; dusty, auburn, charcoal—

like a brush—

swirls and dashes, bristles painting beauty

in browns.

or a child

chocolate on his fingers, wiping

smudges on once-clean shirt:

art.

he laughs, face sticky splotches.

it's what i see here:

plywood—

cut and broken pieces glued together

a collage of misfits makes

a castle of might.

and maybe it's like me, us,

lives brought together,
stories written
through a Creator God
who is making all things new
and beautiful
like chocolate stains.

# freedom

i heard the word "freedom"
but i wasn't free
—like thinking of colors
when i couldn't see—
like reading a sentence
again in my head,
but when i am finished
don't know what it said.
i heard the word "freedom"
and prayed it to be
something to clothe me,
my reality.

then God gave me freedom
and helped me to see
before the beginning

He chose and knew me.
His grace is a free gift
i don't have to earn;
He knows all yet chose me
i love Him in turn.
like i was an orphan,
was lost and inept
and He was a Father
a place for me kept.

i don't have to worry
to do the right things,
His grace is sufficient
that's why my heart sings.
i've never been freer
or saw with such light
when resting in Jesus
and Him my delight.

like reading a sentence
someone holds my hand,
whispers the meaning:
now i understand.
and dear heart that's weary
you too can be free.
there's hope and assurance,
His glory for me.

# heart questions

can a beating heart still be lifeless
like a new fallen tree yet in green
spirit alive
but living a lie
heart that is beating unseen?

can a smile upturned still be heavy
as the sunshine is darkened by rain
they turn aside
and something dear dies
lips in a smile or pain?

can a face without flaw still be broken
like a storm that thrashes the sea
does beauty suffice
frozen in ice

drowning, and yet she can't flee?

can one who is rich still have nothing
leaves tossed away in a gale
clasping at air
hopes only tear
it too will finally fail?

can one hope for something eternal
a reason to push through the night
eyes that are kind
mercy to find
adorning softly in light?

heart beat anew,
beauty that's true
storm no longer blinding our sight.

# home

do you ever have that ardent passion

to be Home?

not that this earthly home is utterly marred or bad

for there's good here too—

but ahh, the good of Home is better,

best of all.

for there, the trees are my trees,

the flowers familiar,

the noises a lullaby to this lonely heart.

the streets and faces are smiling,

and my special spots of quiet await.

every single place is lit up like fairy glitter

by the knowing of Him.

to be Home!

yet to know, He is waiting at Home

He will bring it down to this home-like place,

make it real.

how can i wait?

i step into

the autumn's breath of fog—

early morning, cold and wet and still

yet bugs still sing, deceived by night's lingering.

the night is hazy glass,

blurred grey everywhere,

but close, i see color—

the pink of a rose edged in droplets

the clouds cannot hide.

i see no trees or hills or sky but

expanseless ash, and only here—

with me—i see color.

it reminds me of Home.

until geese call,

the fog shatters in whooshing air,

and black bodies cut through the void.

unafraid, slicing the greyness,

searching for Land beyond.

this morning, i do too:

one step, cold grass by my feet.

another, limping forward.

but color moves with me, here in this cloud all along;

i step into fog, find clearness

because Truth shatters this deception, and

on the other side of darkness

morning wakes,

and a Land awaits with forever color.

# it's gonna be alright

i am dancing in faith,

and they might think me crazy

to stand in night's utter darkness,

silence of foreboding time,

and feel a song in my soul:

*it's gonna be alright.*

endlessly lonely years

and lingering of winter frost,

yes, i hurt and feel the numbness, icy wind blasts

—no bother—

this faith is believing in what i can't see.

i'm confident

that morning will dawn again.

His promises are true:

to expel this night by the light of a coming King and a Kingdom,
and in this shadow
i am fully loved, forgiven, known
like noon sun's embrace, kisses.


*it's gonna be alright.*


i have a little faith He gave,
and He is faithful:
worthy of belief,
the sun that is always shining, even at night
when i can't see.
He is a Father holding me gently and whispers,
*sleep, child, i have you.*
i may wake to morning stars
or thick darkness yet,
but maybe
—hope against hope—
it'll be Day.
*soon*, He promises,
and that's enough.
i'm dancing in faith, and they might think me crazy.
if only they knew the song,


*it's gonna be alright.*
because of Him.

# oracles

those Words that once surrounded me

like nothing else could;

that quilt, warmer

than all the rest and my favorite

colors, together.

i read those Words, wistful heat

till autumn waned.

and i lost them.

not the Words—the wonder,

whimsical wonder of childhood

i forgot

like the holes in my quilt.

i'm a flower, dying.

the Words hold nothing

yet everything.

i can't escape.

but the quilt draws a breath,
warmth, despite the worn edges
and those Words wait to surround me—
colors, thoughts of spring.
promises that i need, desperate,
and remember
when i go back.

# renewed

i want to live as an eagle

high, unafraid

soaring on gently curved wings

that are black, like the night

yet slice through the dawn.

i want to fly

as if the storms are merely a moment

and wind carries me, a breath.

i'm still, gliding,

never looking down

or changing my course.

because where the heavens meet the earth

i'm free

trusting in something—*Someone*—bigger than myself.

sweeping through gales,

riding on the breeze,

eagle eyes on the horizon

and holding onto the promise like wind:

i'm renewed.

if i ever fall

i'll just get up

and keep

flying.

# shaped by the future

looking back is like slipping into a ballroom gown.
i step into Truth, transformed
by a Man who loved fully, lived fully too
and gave all to die for me.
He washed me from a sinner to a saint
(or a pauper to a princess),
and looking back, i'm ready to dance.

but if i never looked forward, how sure could i step;
i'd slip on the ribbons, fall when i leapt
'cause the Man who laid down was received once again,
and i know i shall too.

so i dance for a Kingdom that will not pass away,
and my spins are for riches never to fade
may my footwork be sure

my slippers grow worn
for the day this princess receives a crown
and lays it
at the Man's feet.

may i dance
for the day i rise.
may i look forward
to resurrection.

# shattering darkness

complete darkness,

stillness

of an empty world, the surface of the deep.

midnight breaks by a shard of

l i g h t

piercing the void

as the foundations of the earth are laid. deep waters measured but

being pushed back, bars and doors.

brilliant gold in first dawning sun and

morning stars singing together:

a melody, awakening life.

roaring from the new dwelling of light, darkness

flees to its place.

treasuries of snow, hail

lay their head and wait

listening for first command.

east wind scatters across

hills, endless plains of earth,

fingers of air following their order

until pierced—

path for the thunderbolt.

heavenly power displayed, yet silenced

smallest stars known by name

and holding dominion.

beasts born quiet, teeth still

eyes turning upward to

the silent serenade of earth

and all pause to listen.

the Voice that called them forth

eyes of fire, lips

of mercy.

One who shattered darkness

into burning light.

# silence of the day

i never knew quiet hid in wide daylight,

like standing in a street, cars

flashing noise i don't hear, looking up.

only peace, that peace.

when sun shines, life alive, i hear quiet

because when it sets, sounds explode with crickets and frogs and

bugs,

and it rises to the chorusing of birds' praise;

how can i sleep?

perhaps daylight hushes to hear *my* song

to let this soul sing its starring role,

and i will sleep again.

may i praise when the sun shines, quiet

and wait in noises exploding this earth.

sing or rest to prepare for the Promised Land

and set my soul on the Man of praise.

## something crazy

i'll do something crazy
    one day
      which no one will understand.
  like setting sail and stepping
        out
      on the water
        and walking,
           eyes always up
             treading on waves.
i'll do something crazy
  like selling all i own
      giving the rest away
      and embarking
    on a journey no one has returned from.
       climb the highest mountain
      explore the coldest tundra

see through the thickest fog.

i'll do something crazy

something extraordinary

in this world of

ordinary.

sameness.

safety.

i'll be different

somehow.

'cause there's something

deep inside me

that's bigger

than this whole world,


and it needs to   e  s  c  a  p  e.

# some things never change

i'm not who i thought i would be
about to become an adult;
fanciful dreams, different reality
the girl who would smile
charming face, perfect grace.
thought i'd be braver, bolder, more beautiful,
but i'm still me.
i'm scared of the future
alone, still timid and shy, still
flawed with scars.
and somehow i'm not
the person i thought i would be.

yet it's okay, i'm not
afraid when my eyes are set
on more.

my Lord and King, Creator

of eternity, the one who knows

the stars, creates

the wind, writes

my story despite the sin;

He is.

i wish i was braver, bolder, more

beautiful. but i'm still

me

and God is God.

that never changed.

# wait, dear heart

have you ever seen that cloud your eyes are drawn to?

a billowing, white mountain of a giant

or sturdy pillar of marble,

towering, standing higher and higher?

tonight, it lit up

lightning-orange sears in whiteness:

a storm far away

approaching.

if i sat and watched, a lifetime

to wait, but no.

i tear myself away, eyes close in rest.

it's okay.

i believe the shower will come,

and that's enough.

oh, dear heart of mine, so restlessly

striving to patiently wait,

breathe.

do you believe in your Father,

will He not bring forth a shower?

to wait is like tearing eyes away

and believing we'll still dance in the rain.

# wistful gusts

they said i could not see the wind
from where it came or why
but when i pause and raise my eyes
soft snow is slipping by.
it twirls and dances in the sky
like ballet slippers flying high
spinning whiteness, all around,
am i not seeing wind?

they said i could not hold the wind
it slips through fingers so,
but my hands clutched a flying kite
kept wind where it would go
scarlet and orange against the blue
air in my face, i steered it true
skyborne kite, banner of mine

am i not holding wind?

they said i could but hear the wind
the hardest one thus far—
ears turned away, run through the day
wind's music but a mar
i slipped away from all to find
to hear, to make a treasure mine
of zephyr's song, just beyond
for now i'm hearing wind.

# witness of twilight

first star slashing through twilight pink,
and it's all i see.
silver shine then gone like a sword
paused in peace—a shooting star.
yet 'twas the tiniest revealing of the heavens beyond
or mirror reflecting a ray of the place
where the light Maker reigns:
that throne room of glory
as light explodes like thunder.
from that reality to ours, in stars' witness.
a sky of blue-grey, dusk, with scales of clouds
like fish swimming into a pool of glassy sunset,
and their tails—more clouds linger, metallic
by an orange moon
that reflects a sun i can't see.
beauty

glory

peace

i inhale it all, the way a shooting star was a witness

to her Maker

in a world ebbing black yet light,

and i think of the throne room

tonight.

# thorns

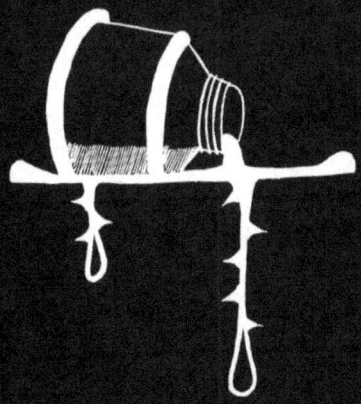

hope in His promise despite present pain

# a look not taken

i never thought a world could change in a look not taken, until he
didn't.
a lost glance, and our cars hit like a rocket,
shatter, thrown forward,
that crushing noise,
then stillness.
breathe in. release.
if he had looked but once.

but Father, help me not do the same,
not meet a gaze then deflect
and never truly see a hurting soul;
not miss a silent cry for help,
or fail to love the one right in front of me.
Father, may You through me bring healing,
the slowing of traffic, open windows to breathe,

teach me to see,

teach me to take that look.

# apparition, i know not

this fog is a mirage of ashy grey:

smoke drifting from long-dead fire,

transparent yet sickening the air.

even that haze is broken

being washed away by the rain's tears:

continual drips on my window

blotting out the light, staining.

too dull for silver, too lifeless for blue,

that grey mist that covers.

a thick blanket,

and i sprawl, choke, try

to breathe

as the universe descends;

i'm trapped

in that grey.

there are memories of color

like the blue that once caressed my skies

or the way trees shone emerald before fall stole their breath.

leaves fell. clouds came. i'm choked

by this smoke.

were the colors real or is this mirage,

this greyness,

the reality that's choking me

in raindrops?

# appomattox

oh Father, i look for worship, somewhere
in virginia mountains of rolling green,
tumbling shadows into the rippled lake,
and autumn turns, cool kiss on my cheeks,
but i cry—do You?

oh Father, the grassy glens drank blood
as they fought from the ridge to this house;
last shots fired tore life through chests,
and men died.
gunpowder and blood, that smell.
today's all green, but i see it,
and where was worship, was goodness there?

dear Father, but one last cry i beg—
as moon sits in Your virginia sky and horizon glows feebly—

like the night after the courthouse.
men cheered, dreams died, night came anyway,
and a general rode sad to his bedraggled troops
who died for a forgone cause.


was worship there as they met their brothers
broken on that railroad trail, last regiment
setting bayonets high, last salute, surrender,
and former enemies greeted them with these cheers?
was worship in that brotherhood,
that chivalrous kindness,
that moment?
they mourned and bravely surrendered
between the line of trees and open field.


i cry, my Father.
and in this moment,
i worship.

Nicole ElsieRose

# battlefront revelation

sun reflects on polished armor
like silver eyes stalking its prey
arrows sharpened for the kill
slice the air, race for my heart

i am unarmed, my body still
swords clash with resounding fury
slices, parries, thrusts—nearer and nearer
two sides close around me
grabbing me in their sharp talons

the wind catches hold of my hair
sweeping back until i face the enemy
two armies surround me
and my hands hang empty
i could grasp at the wind

but it would slip through my fingers

the battle deafens me, blinds my vision
i forget who i am, lost in the moment
sound and light are one resounding thunderclap
the war raging within my soul

'til out of the darkness, a white steed breaks
through the battle with flowing mane
hooves rear up and paw the air
the fight sounds around us
two armies intertwined in a war
struggle for a victory that will never come

the horse quivers
strong eyes flash
they search for a white banner
but the horizon is broken only by blood
the knight astride reaches down a hand
my arms surround him

and i am swept away, heart against heart
swords disappear, and arrows fall short
we gallop into the mountains, jagged peaks
leaving the war cries behind

forever forward, forever up

'til the battle fades within me
here in the presence of my savior
i surrender all
for i am saved

# beyond procellous

stormy, as the sea

this world, this heart.

lies slashing like rain, thunder of the enemy,

but this soul is beyond procellous.

the ocean is a vapor,

and You, my rock, are still.

beneath the seas is calmness

and above the clouds, silence.

only this moment, present time, is a storm,

and i dive in

to reach the bedrock, eyes set

through troubled waters.

You are beyond procellous

You are Victor

the battle already won; storm silenced

by mere mention of You, Lord,

and Your sword will divide the waters.
save us,
and draw me to Your bosom at last.
i dive, swim,
eyes set on Truth beyond this time
the storm has no hold on me.
beyond procellous:
You, victorious, holy One

# bursting forth

they think i am perfect
brave one they look up to
strong enough to face
the darkness
and burn it with unquenchable
light.
but it sears me, and i'm left
dry, a desert or wasteland
parched ground and thirsty land

i'm afraid.
i'm broken. and
i'm weak.

it never stopped Him.

my dryness bubbles into a pool,
cool reflections in gentle drops.
my wasteland bursts into grass:
reeds and rushes
rejoicing in life.
my parched ground turns soft
and blossoms as the rose
abundantly.


they think i am perfect
but i'm not.
He is,
and i am desperate
for His life.

Lisa Elis

# caducous

falling early

so i gather littering leaves, faint hues

green almost yellow,

ruby not yet turned

like an empty life or a sunrise hidden

behind ashy clouds.

run, wish i could press them again to the trees,

instead fall, turn to humus,

empty rainforest crying

like dancers bent in tears.

i'll practice, stretch, expand my lungs

to blow away grey morning clouds,

gather leaves, throw—

chance for just one more day of autumn.

and love,

embrace,

and cry and pray

for hearts to not fall early,

years to stretch on, empty,

but for just

one

more

day

to dream and believe in a Purpose bigger than themselves

and that a Kingdom really is coming.

# condensation

a million flecks of white
as if Heaven sneezed
in crystal glitter.
i could sit here forever, watching,
gazing out the window.
thin sheet of white
with sprigs of green
and autumn's leaves peeking through.
trees with velvety, soft hats
and even this window lined
with condensation.
i never liked that word,
as it felt stuffy, overbearing, but today it's beautiful
in droplets.
a snowflake catches on the glass,
and it's a perfect flower with six petals

all icy, cold flecks.

i breathe,

stain the window

almost smell frozen air and tender flakes

innumerable.

## dear irah,

i only saw you for a
minute. the way
your dark eyes caught mine,
deep in your caramel skin, smooth
like an ocean's palm,
and that one wave washed you away—
pulled me from you.
i'm waiting on this sand, hot
on my soles, but i can't see you
anymore.
so i whisper across the expanse
hope you hear, somehow:

> *you're beautiful, deep inside*
> *in the image of Him,*
> *and He has purpose*
> *bigger than you imagine.*

one last whisper:

*you're loved.*

*always*

my reflection watches me,

flecks of silver in blue waters;

i wonder if you see yours

or hear my words

though we met for but

a minute.

and i think of all those other eyes

that met mine,

the souls who brushed my shoulder

and were gone in an instant;

why does life have strangers?

my message is for them too,

for everyone listening,

for you:

*you're loved.*

*always.*

*have Hope,*

*a Kingdom is coming.*

# dear one

when you were young, you sang
to Me, but you didn't know
I listened.
you grew up and ran
the pace of life,
endless train on stretching track
until it crashed.
life as you knew it
was smashed and broken,
altered forever.
you ran from Me,
saying it was My fault,
that I had abandoned you.
but how could I help you
when you pushed Me away
and trampled My love like ash?

you thought you were alone.
but I was still there—
leading, guiding, calling,
ever stretching out My hand,
the hand you never took.
I am a lover; I won't
let you go.
I'll keep waiting
and loving.
maybe one day you'll give up,
give in and take My hand
for I never grow tired
of waiting,
My dear one.

# eternity's glow

i'm scared.

hurting and lost,

and i don't know how to find it:

the thing i need.

i'm looking for it, for something,

but it slips between my fingers

like darkness with a handful of stars,

and i would reach up, grab one

clasp it in my arms

if only that could stop the hurt.

but the stars laugh, too far away,

and i fall

again.

i want to fix it,

paint the night in white glows

until the whole celeste is a glowing sphere

one star to swallow up all the blackness.

but i can't.

every day ends,

night comes,

and i am stuck in the darkness

searching for the stars, but sometimes

i only find empty skies.

so i remember every night has a morning

every sky, a basket of stars

even when i can't see them

or when they're far away.

they're always there,

and always is a word that lasts forever

like *eternity*

and *forgiveness*

and maybe even *hope*.

hope tries to slip through my hands, and i can't hold on,

i let go and whisper for help.

eyes up, for maybe the stars shine for a purpose

for hope

a hope i don't understand

but i want.

if i'm still scared, still hurt

it will be okay

if Someone will hold me

and remind me that hope lives on,

because it will become Reality.

# extramundane

i wish i could see it…

or do i?

a vine tangled, winding up,

grasping to trees like straws,

twined: me to this age i sink into.

oh, for a hatchet to sever me, to see once

Him.

all beauty and color and joy beyond

this world in one to come.

beyond the moment, the shadows, today.

beyond the mundane,

further up, further in.

extra—that One

His name destroys all yet calls

in Love.

sever me! cut me loose!

let me trade this universe for Him,

all-consuming One

who will purge it and restore what was broken as whole.

my heart's fiery yearning

combats my heart's deepest fear.

dare i wish to see it?

# exposed

today i flee from summer's eyes

to where the forest folds me in his shadows—

mine disappears in his,

and i feel safe.

from that light, heat, exposing and knowing

all of me.

but i can't.

here in grey trunks and flat leaves and empty ground,

even here, light is.

it exposes beauty:

a snapped twig—not grey

but mauve, purple under minty moss and golden fungus.

i peel away, inside like a chestnut mare

dancing on shodden hooves

or like Kentucky clay a child plays in.

deeper, the wood's inner vein, sandy brown.

the leaves too, textured,

rounded tops of glass and underbellies seamed

all revealed in this sunlight.

a ground of twining ferns and

fallen walnuts, some cracked from collision

ready to stain my fingers; still beauty

and me

here,

hiding yet exposed by a light

that never stops pursuing and finding all of me

yet knowing who i was meant to be.

kind of like Jesus.

# first frost

they said everything died last night
in frozen fingers,
          murderous ice
stealing life and cutting deep
with wintery knives,
and I hurt, cried
because it was true.

in darkness, shadows grew
and silence
          too.

but this morning, i heard birds singing
and a thread of sunshine
turning the silver world into golden tapestries
and crystal gems.

i won't cry
i'll sing.

memories are beautiful
and darkness is slain in light's illuminance.
today's the best day of my life,
because Jesus
          is here, in me

even in
this ice.

# goodbye

i say it:
> *goodbye*

but it still hurts, like last time did.
or like the skyline

                              before

                                        the

                                    sun

                            goes

                    down.

bubbles—violet, scarlet, turquoise too
all gone, popped—or crushed—
to **blackness.**

                                  i don't cry.

                                  just stare

                                      up

at stars 'til they

fade too.

goodbye, i whisper and

remember

to savor

every                moment  FOREVER.


or at least try.

the horizon,

the    b u b b l e s

are gone

but that's okay.

the light

i still grasp

and dance


to       catch       every       disappearing       bubble       ,


He gives me Hope.

# higher vision

vibrant hues of scarlet-pink sweep
like the fingers of a brush on canvas.
paint smears from sunset horizon and upwards
twirling through the clouds, a masterpiece
only God could create.
rainbows of violet lace—
the edge of the mountains
snowy heads always gazing up
looking, searching for the stars
unaware that their feet rest in forests.
pine trees wear caps of white;
icy flakes stroke their boughs
until slipping down
to rest
on a soft forest floor of snow,
frozen blades died away:

the warmth of the past.

because unless they die, they cannot live again,

and this is their silent song, and ours.

the trees and mountains look ever

upward, seek the light

light of a day when all things

will be made new.

# i shall not want

she stumbles, falls,
and her palms are marked
with blood, like the bruises
she tries to hide.
tears fall,
stain her cheeks, she tries
to stand, yet falls
again.
a hand reaches.
it's Him; she turns away,
but His palm touches her—
touches the blood
and lifts,
gentle.
she winces, waits,
covers the bruises another man gave

and pulls her shoulders tight.

His fingers squeeze, a whisper:

*—it's okay—*

His eyes are blue

and smile, somehow

as she sees His hands

silent around hers

and He stands and leads her.

rocks fade to grass.

the soft, dirt path that disappears—

silent waters.

it washes her fingers

blood stains, clean,

and a light mist falls

like stars.

she smells clean earth,

feels those hot tears

and His hands, firm.

*—it's okay—*

# it won't be too long now

goodbyes
are like a mountain range
too far off in the distance,
and it makes my stomach tight,
gives a bad taste in my mouth.

but somehow, goodbye is all
i got.
so i give it fiercely
with love choked in my strangling hug
and whisper-cry
of, "in a little while."
i want to climb those mountains.
so i hope.

# life's colliding colors

*crimson.*

the poppies that grow in the spring
and listen to the old bell ring.
brick houses line our every street
where chimneys billow, fire heat.
old pictures hung on every wall
near telephones that used to call—
their memories folded, tucked away
from cheeks now white, the red astray.

*jade.*

before the sun set long ago
on grass that peeks through trampled snow,
the leaves that lingered through the frost
green sprigs that froze with summer lost.

soft beads that hung upon her neck
the way her cheeks with color fleck,
'til snow closed in and stole her breath,
her face pale blue; eyes closed in death.

*ivory.*
the snow so white and yet still cold
ices the window, world to fold
yet bursting open through the door
feet running out, missing the floor.
when resurrection's in her eyes
pink kiss her cheeks as soft snow flies.
a King will come and raise this all
where past and present both now fall.

# live

it's the Live:
everyday moments that are windows
to something greater, beyond
like early morning.
i see a spiderweb spun in gold
pure, gilded alloy
little filaments, floating and dancing
in sunshine,
and clouds laughing off cold roofs when heat bursts,
tickles of fog running away
and brushing the spider's web—
i wonder if she sees and loves it too?

the gold is like His Kingdom's streets
the foggy clouds—His Spirit, presence,
and two world meet: today and the forever future.

let me live it—

## lost one

give up, please
give in. you are
burning, inferno of red
heat that sears you
sears my heart as i watch.
i reach out. grab my hand
even if it hurts, i beg you
give up, please give in.

you said you were strong enough,
but you don't realize
i don't ask
for strength.
brokenness
is okay.
and one day,

that strength will fail
falling deeper into the fire
crashing, burning, alone without
hope. please
come back to me.
i'm the gentle mist
to cool your hurt, soft
breeze to caress your heart
if you only give up.

please give in
because i love you.

# oceanicity

the waves lap gentle, lick the shore

singing a song of times forgotten,

but soon they too will forget the melody.

i see sand and trees, breeze quivering through—

they laugh, dancing to a song of their own imagination.

do they know my past,

the pain, the hurt, the tears?

can they read my thoughts?

they just live life, reaching for the sun.


and i am alone.

i don't need them.

i am strong enough.


leaves tower high; i am lost.

i am like a wave, stolen away

by the ocean's icy fingers.

but something else is pulling on my heart;

in this place, i hear Someone call my name.

the voice is a mere whisper on the wind

but stretches across the sea.

dare i answer?

# one month later

before one month ago, the roses bloomed,
and i loved it:
the crimson-pink, softness as i smelled,
nose against petal, inhaling.
sweet,
before the first snow came.
frost killed those blooms—
withering, lingering,
trying to hold on as they died.
roses edged in ice.
that month ago, they laughed.
now i cry
for what's lost.
even when ice thaws, it returns
and hurts again,
freezes my petals.

i try to dance, but it's cold;
i see my breath, slip on frost,
and cry again.
so many days ago, innocent life
yet the snow falls, and i try
to dance.
because one day spring will come,
and i'll understand why.

# only a candle

the wick sinks low, silent flame quivers,
one breath of air whispers through,
and i am gone,
a memory.
no warmth, no light
continual stillness, life stolen by death.

what would my days have meant?
would someone miss me, shedding tears
longing for one last moment together?
or would life go on,
birds still sing and sun still shine,
life being lived without me?
another candle could be lit
to fill the void i left,
hours slipped between my fingers.

but as i rejoice in the Kingdom
i hope that someone would sigh,
"this young girl drew me to Jesus' arms,
and i have a reason to live."

if only one heart was brightened
by the glow His fire had lit
it would be worth all
the pain, the tears;
my life would have been well lived.

yet still the sun shines warm,
and birds sing in the trees;
another day, a life to live
to laugh, to cling, to love.

a day is but a memory
'til it becomes
something more.

# out of bounds

Father, You tease me to play
like i did as a child, counting to twenty
then running, seeking
for the friends in playful hiding.
every forgotten tree or bush or corner held a secret
as *ready or not* became a challenge,
and we laughed as we ran or argued
because someone was out of bounds.
we're like butterflies flitting in colored dance.
Father, You invite me to play
Saying, *My playground's this earth*
*and you can search from the east to west.*
so i do.
from jungle mountains and skyscraper cities of asia,
the arid, aussie air,
to norwegian fjords, edged with cliffsides,

california beaches where surfers ride,

and depths of undiscovered ocean valleys—volcanoes bubble.

i search, the corners of Your world

to the center

where jerusalem waits with walled cities and memories in every

crag, anticipating.

ready or not, i never find it:

the sins You've forgiven.

my mistakes and ugliness and who i was before You

it's gone.

out of bounds.

You laugh and draw me into Your arms,

and this forgiven girl throws herself in.

how i love You, Father,

so i dance and live in the freedom You give

when we play hide and seek together.

# overthrown

great stones bow down, pink
in the dawning sun:
the sun that rises
on the once majestic ruins.
the barricades kneel low under a shadow
last elm standing strong after so many years
remembering glory now past.


among the rubble, ivy interlaces,
emerald vines twined together,
like the hand of a maiden clinging to her lover.
eyes lock in silent promise,
lips tight under flushed cheeks
fingers melt together, soft head against chest.
melody only they could hear
swaying under the ever-knowing elm.

the lover slips a white lily to the maiden
a blooming vow, now gracing her tresses
and auburn curls pushed back with his kiss.
heart races, lips tremble,
but he pulls away as a knight.
she gives him away.

gloves on his hands, breastplate covering heart
a steed awaits and paws the ground—
the dust that sweeps him away forever.
far from the castle, horse stumbles
sword falters, and he gives his last breath
for a King.

under the elm, she waters the ground
with tears, embrace the dust.
tender fingers clutch a pure lily white,
a last remaining memory
until that too fades away.

fortress fell to ivy's cold fingers
interlaced as years take its toll.
birds mock the past wonder, fly towards the sun,
now setting in twilight,
but an elm watches all
remembering the tears of a maiden

her gown soft on his roots.

a love that seemed lost, but also
a promise:
a Kingdom would come again.
and the King is worthy.

# potsherd

my sunbaked skin would burn

even after all those days in blistering heat,

and i worried that

one day it'd turn

crunchy, heel of a loaf, gagging.

so i ran, always ran

to where forest tickled field and deeper

where water waited

silent pools amid twirling eddies

and me in the middle

wading 'til my toes turned to raisins

fingertips too

curled and soft and bumpy.

and i found treasure, no one else knew

where water splashed its scents:

little forgotten stones, bits

of pottery and pots and plates, long ago

my collection now.

something the sun could never steal:

rippled pottery of blue,

a gently-curved smile of brown

with little flowers.

i was scolded for wasted time

mud in my hair, grit in my mouth,

my bleeding feet on thorny ground when i left,

yet no one knew the hidden museum i found

except the One

the One i knew who must have

put it all there

for me.

gems hidden from this

sunbaked world.

## sand table

i always had this picture:
of rose-gold sand with sparkles
like gems in the sunlight.
grubby hands grabbing, tossing up
and a yellow rain of sandy goodness,
gold dust,
and laughter.
and the water, there
together yet apart.
shining clearness, cold, and pure,
one could see their face and a hundred
clouds peeking in,
and the smell
like a drizzle in a rainforest
or fog on a cool night.

but my picture is gone, and a new one

found. everything together—mixed.

sand in the water,

dirty hues of brown like messy hands,

muddy feet,

and no reflection, only blurs

where gold and water should be.

and that outside smell of wet hair and mud.


i see it here in the sand table and in life:

confusions, mixing of sand and water,

and i'm weak and uncertain.

but when i ask, He's there

making my moats of mud into sandcastle palaces.

He asks for trust:

i do.

when i don't understand, He tells me

what i need for today,

and i've never been happier.

even if this picture wasn't what i imagined—

as a child is dunked in a hot bubble bath,

sandy grit mixing with bubbles—

it's beautiful,

so beautiful.

# supercilious

this world, this air—

biting breath of frost, like winter

grabs autumn's leaves and shoves them in her pocket

stifled in her hands, dies

gasping breath found no life.

hateful, hurtful,

dissentious—

this world full of quarrels

and disappeared Love

where bothers reign as queen, icy

like winter.

we hurt.

and yet there's a morn' every sunrise and

hope

hope

beautiful hope.

we're carried above it all, flying
in wings of hope like eagles
sunrays delighting leafless branches,
a soul sings.

# the distance

i'm stumbling forward in this darkness,

rain that slices my skin

pelts my eyes with ice.

it's cold, i cry

for help, for someone, anyone

to just hear

care

come…

but only this thundering storm of tears,

this ache within me

that burns, clenches tight.

my fingers are frost.

i can't escape

or run fast enough, far

enough to leave this shadowed world.

so i stop,

raise my eyes,

and there i see it,

like that first morning star

after a night thick and endless.

or the warmth of a blanket

soft as i escape the snow,

smell of ginger and hot chocolate.

even if distant, a hope.

hope of something to rescue me,

Someone.

so i cry,

but run

always forward

with my eyes set.

even if rain blinds me, i'll keep running

because nothing can stop

that hope.

# the secret of the thinking tree

the sounds, the lights, are blinding me,
a storm that crashes deafening.
with every bolt, i cry anew
and wish that someone really knew
or took the time to see.

they say, *i love you* and, *i care*
but if they knew, they'd only stare
and turn away, pretending that
beside this sin they never sat,
because it's only fair.

and so i run into the rain,
my candle dying with the pain
until i thrust it on a tree
the candlestick that waits for me

to light the one door frame.

i push it open, step inside—
tree boughs a haven i can hide
where I can think and talk and be
an orphan with a family
and here i can abide.

i'm not alone, 'cause He is here
and loves me true despite my fear,
for in this place i hide away
to hear Him speak, *with you I stay*
if only i draw near.

if they could know or even see
the way He fixes broken me
they all would run right through the storm
this secret tree where He can form
our lives like pottery.

this is the secret that I know:
seeds that look dead can somehow grow,
and broken pots can be made new;
when doors are opened, He comes through.
to love despite rain's flow.

# this celebration

the kitchen has been invaded by so many
bowls and pots, spoons and spills
all under those dozen hands trying at once,
those legs going back and forth
up since so early
this morning. craziness:
there's music and laughter,
a little voice begging to help,
creative messes forming
a feast.
but stepping back, a hole.
one bowl unattended, two eggs,
waiting and watching the empty apron
there on the wall.
blue, with red roosters,
but they don't crow, all waiting.

it's like that puzzle, one piece missing

long gone, but we still search

under tables, in cabinets

his favorite hiding places

empty.

we keep rushing, cooking, trying to not remember

but we remember anyway.

sometimes i think i hear his laugh

then it's gone

again.

this bittersweet celebration,

we try to rejoice

even though our puzzle

is missing a piece.

it'll be okay

one day

when Jesus comes home.

Brooklyne Elysse

# under the crimson roses

bells chime around me,

perfect unison with each drop of rain.

gray skies release their flood winds,

torrents drowning the cobblestones beneath.

but I am safe here

under an umbrella of crimson roses.

sweet fragrance surrounds me,

blossoms laughing in the mist.

rain kisses the petals, embraces tight

and slips away

until hovering at the edge.

each droplet clings, shimmering

like a crystalline diamond.

waiting, watching, whispering

they fall down,

down

until shattering on the stones
wet against my bare feet.
another drop falls, continual tears,
yet I am safe under the whispering bells.
lonely streaks of rain line the umbrella,
crimson roses looking down
to diamonds broken at my feet.

# voices, those voices

my life is a forest,

that's what they see, but don't.

it's like a poem, those elegant words,

but they never know how the pencil stumbled,

pen fell, paper tore

the ugly behind the beauty

like the forest i am.

when they hear my boughs in the wind

they think i'm singing

or laughing

they think the wind makes me dance.

but what if i'm crying

and those gusts are tearing off my branches

making me bleed,

fall,

crash?

they see the lush canopy i hide in

and think i'm a princess

just dreaming away in my palace home,

those emerald leaves like gems

sparkling in my hair.

but what if

behind the first layer

my branches crack,

leaves tumble to the floor

trampled, rotting into mush?

a palace hall where i'm alone.

do i dance like they say? or am i lost,

hiding, wandering,

but wishing someone would find me?

my life is this forest

scented with cedar and honeysuckle

and those wildflowers that peek into the thickets,

but their blooms have thorns, and i smell the storm

that wind that tears me in its gale.

it's coming harder, faster.

maybe i'll play in the raindrops

or be torn by the hail.

they think i'm a hero

but i'm not.

i'm just broken, searching

for the beauty beyond the brokenness

the way the thorns flower,

the leaves cover,

wind laughs,

and there

i try to dance anyway

not to show them or prove myself

but because i'm searching

for that beauty.

# blossoms

love's action of loyalty until budding,
we can be with Him

# airplanes on the clouds

i hear a gentle call to *worship,*

and i could jump up and dance

—feet airplanes on the clouds—

or write in elegant poetry or wordsmith riddles.

i could pour out fragrance from alabaster jars,

paint in sweeping colors,

or climb a mountain and sit in wonder—

maybe blowing bubbles and giggling like a lass.

ahh, i must worship,

because this love for You urges me to give the highest gift—

wonder that You see me

and trade my sins for Jesus' righteousness,

wonder that You invite me into your very near presence

even today.

so in this moment, i worship.

not grandiose,

magnificent,

not fitting of a King.

but i worship with a colored pencil

on paper crisp with dry paint and child scribbles

as i simply love a baby in my arm.

she'll wake and never remember—

tiny fuchsia lips, little veins through near translucent skin,

grunts and wiggles in her sleep,

and her hair is fuzzy from yesterday's bath.

the blackboard is smudged from another day's art,

and the toddler wiggles beside me for a story to read.

i don't have an alabaster jar

or gold or riches.

legs curl up, not in dance,

so i offer my words in a simple act

whispering, *i love You*

and worship in baby and toddler snuggles

today.

maybe tomorrow worship will be my feet dancing

like airplanes on the clouds.

# all in the open

i found You, Father, hiding all in the open—

or You let Yourself be found.

in rolling storm clouds, flag snapping

with fierce kisses of the wind,

and my hair flies.

but i see You, Father.

rain pours in sheets and leaves,

mist, across blanketed earth, sunset pierces the grey

orange gold on crying earth

and You, Hope, i cling.

then tree shadows, sun flickers as a candle.

i see the slivered moon

climb above the horizon silhouettes, still in fog

a planet pretends to twinkle but brighter.

smell of dinner ready, but i'm lost;

here in sweetly-thick mist

i see You.

enamored, amazed,

i could dance; it's called Joy.

You've been hiding in the open

all along.

and i wonder if You were waiting for me

to just look.

Tarissa Hughes

# asunder

i never thought i'd glimpse

ocean waves lapping before me,

mist rolling, tumbling head over head,

white spray

i inhale.

grass and wind and sunshine

and glitter falls from heaven.

maybe we're fairies

and this, our flowery meadow.

so many dreams.

if i open my eyes, i'll see

that waves are seedheads

of grass

rolling like billows in the wind.

that glitter is pollen

and spores.

and we're loved people in a broken world,

He bids us become who He made us to be.

dreams, reality

dancing on ocean waves

and mist. fairy mist.

# bubble

two ruby lips pucker up—

a wisp of air,

the child points and giggles

as wind sweeps away the glowing sphere.

yellows and reds reflect

like autumn trees on a silent lake

until even they disappear.

the child slips away unseen

not knowing that the full beauty comes

beyond the eyes of man

and under the gaze of the clouds.

because there the bubble still flies with unified colors—

a rainbow glittering like jewels.

the colors swirl and dance

silk slippers of ballerinas

dancing to the song of the wind.

and sometimes i wonder
if i reached up towards the crystal globe
would i touch a piece of heaven
and be swept away into the glory.

Treasure Happy

# butterfly tendrils

i saw her:

a mark, blot on the earth

flitting creature, a penny size,

but a name He gives her, whisper close:


Beauty—orange flecks on her wings, tendrils purple,

brown like humus under shadow logs,

smell of a rainforest,

colors not in a rainbow, yet one she created.


Dance—as i frighten her perch

injured wings, torn, but they wave,

rise like sunshine, she

twirls, darts, spins

a princess.

Known—purposefully so
for the moment i see her
the forever He does.
her breath may be a wind whisper
but colors a sunset.


He ascribes purpose, beauty, to me
and to this penny size.
fully known, utterly loved
                            somehow.

Brooklyne Elyssie

# cascade higher

cold stone burns

my bare feet, and i stop,

hesitate against black shadows.

leafy ferns cut dark rock,

arching staircase, and i take it—

another step, a ray

like the walkway

that a bride dances through,

higher to arching castle walls.

the white blossoms shake

gentle against her silky train,

and my feet climb higher.

darkness is vanquished by light's sword

sun on my face, lace

against my ankles,

the scent of the ocean

that wisps at my curls.
my eyes rise, misty veil lifted
and i see it—
beyond the tower's wall.
and despite the shadows beneath
white flowers still cascade higher
climbing up,
to explode into the ocean's
endless rays.

.

# crisp world

sweep of brush, the slender fingers

staining clean, white canvas.

forest breeze blows,

leaves dabbed onto invisible trees

that grow, slip into being with colorful sweeps

hesitate, then shadows fall

across crystal lake

soon marred by ripples, stained

by a hungry, noon sun

that cuts the world in rays.

yet blank canvas creeps at the corners

like an invading blizzard;

paintbrush stills,

world dries into being.

fingers wait to dance again

making art to flow from that Love.

# dear new month

first morning, sunrise of You,
whispered promises in premature rays,
i hug them all in.
the clouds are so many "i wonder's"…
of first snows, future tears, fancying joys.
i make goals, dreams,
desires written with heart's pen, most:
to love, to know You, Jesus.

of snows: to frolic with Him there
of tears: to let them wet His heart
of joys: to share and giggle in praise

'tis all, this new month,
only to know i am Yours:
cleaned. washed.
forgiven.

this fair newness in certainty.

# fern

deep, dark dirt peeking

through the fingers of dry leaves:

browns, until color explodes—fireworks

every slender branch grasps

onto a hundred leaves

all lined up.

the firework glows, emerald

large leaves shrivel down,

tiny fingers at the end

they twist, brown with spores,

seeds to fall and carry with it

new life;

until a million leaflets become a carpet—

graceful rug on forest floor

as far as the eye can see

then further.

spiderwebs weave around the stalks

in humid, jungle air

and sounds of faint wind,

but their webs never know

that the forest began with one spore,

one green fern that birthed a hundred

and changed the world

in leafy fireworks.

# fire and ice

i thought the snow was brightest
'til morning came to muse
in shocking gold and crimson,
a battle there to fuse.

a battle like two lovers
with youthful, happy glow
to skip and laugh and chatter
once separate, now they go.

for flakes are soft yet crusty
yet melts like sugar ice
while sunrise comes each morning
forever to entice.

this morn' i saw them marry

reflecting—colors one
like how i'm falling deeper
for Love's already won.


perhaps we're fire and ice and yet
this shocking glows in my skin


and "us" changes me
to who i was always meant to be.

# fire flies

somehow i never saw fireflies before today;

not truly.

they explode the night like fireworks

but silently.

they're the snapping in a fire, yet the air

has never smelled purer.

the sparkle in cold water,

but i am dry yet washed in wonder.

and the fireflies are the glittery dust of fairies,

but there's no magic,

only this Presence of the God who set them in motion—

a dance they've performed ever since.

when i was young, they were lightning bugs

caught in grubby fingers

as I tried to steal what they had

to explode or snap or sparkle like them.

but now

i sit in accompanied darkness, all around

that sweet Presence who made me too,

i see for the first time,

and a deep love has made me

*be* for the first time too.

# flocks of beauties

when sun met clouds
—i saw them both—
sun flying: gold finches
their yellow feathers sleek and
beautiful, spring air, wet grass,
and the birds found white like clouds:
little claws met dandelion stalks.
flowers bent low
into mud.
yellow and white,
sun and clouds
bird pecking off the seeds
one
by
one.
two beauties shining.

i saw them both

meeting like the sky,

then one flitted away to the next

flower.

# goodnight, dreams

*goodnight*

the words are said for the millionth time,

but it's okay somehow

because we keep saying it again.

silence settles in

like the blankets around my shoulders, still warm.

i smell the fresh scent of momma's flowery perfume—

maybe her hair brushed my pillow when she kissed me

or clung to my arms with her hug

when she said, *i love you; sleep tight princess*

and daddy closed the blinds, blew a kiss

and left the door open a crack.

cold feet reach to lay against my legs

i shiver, pull away

but offer an arm instead,

and my little sister curls up next to me.

*tell me a story,* she asks.

i whisper back, *maybe tomorrow,*

but my other sisters heard the words

and we talk again, of games and flowers and friends

of the wedding tomorrow and going to church the next day

to worship in union like we do at home, every day.

we laugh about the cats, the way they looked

when we rubbed pink chalk in their fur.

we giggle quietly,

but daddy still hears us and tells us to sleep

so we try again.

when momma and daddy go to bed, darkness comes.

i pull my blankets close

and shut my eyes,

dreaming of the fireflies outside as i listen to frogs,

how they praise too.

one is loud, by my window—

i wonder if they ever sleep.

sisters snore, the other tugs closer on my arm

and whispers the last *goodnight.*

and i forget to say it back

because i'm already asleep

or at least on the verge of dreams.

# happiness

ah, Father, You are a happy God;

how did i ever not know?

perhaps as i hid in four walls' shadows

sameness—*colors, smells, aloneness*—

i thought only of Your justice,

for You are a Judge, yet what a God of happiness too!


happy—You stuff the world with color

like a child painter—*layers upon layers of vibrance*—

for the sky dances from baby blue to

cerulean and

sunset's merry kisses

with cloud shapes a dreamer laughs and makes pictures from.

earth has a million greens until fall throws her décor

and flowers of every color imaginable.

happy—in innumerable scents
from a porch of petunias' sweet perfume,
the fresh, herb bed of basil and cilantro,
or straw bales in a barn—
horses and sweet feed and saddle tack.
You laugh and even create fragrance in petrichor:
rain drops hitting dry ground.


happy—Your personality bubbling from every creature:
how a friendship causes sweetness
yet a dozen is a montage of uniqueness,
even how one same name is shared with such varied faces!
You mold people who laugh or dream, plan or persevere,
skin and hair and height and persona.
and You also create the smile,
the laugh,
the joke,
the hug.


or in Your animals—
You stretched the neck of the giraffe
and covered her with freckles,
made inchworms smaller than an inch
as they wiggle around,
gave a platypus a bill and webbed feet but no quack,
or made birds that are pink and fly.

how could You not be happy,

overly so?

for it would take all my life to tell

of personalities in tastes

—*richness from so many cultures and countries*—

of how music moves a soul,

or even

of the ultimate joy of being in Your presence

for what joy is from You!


ah yes, You are a judge,

and yet even that is happiness

for You invite me near and whisper,

*you can be forgiven, child*

and draw me into the dance of Your happiness.

# i inhale

i take one breath—

head back, the nostrils open, and chest great

then out.

rest.

gentle air of this morning fog on roses,

dewdrops,

and for a moment, it became part of this body.

that one deliberate breath—

blended with a thousand i never knew—

it was praise, worship.

may the next one be too.

## love spell

i don't understand this:
it's like i'm here, trying
to stand amidst a gale.
the heavens meet earth
in stormy grey and blue and black
swirls and stars of wind
a world outside my own.
yet here it is
       real
       turbulent
       yet soft.
i'm falling
and it surrounds me,
       hugs me
i inhale the fresh wetness
like a dozen daisies under dew drops,
a bed to my soul.

sleeping in this riveting dream of the stars

and will never awake

because heaven met earth

       ethereal

one simply cannot go back.

# moon-like crescents

the light of noon fades away
children laugh, embrace the day;
mothers scold and shake their heads
and birds prepare to make new beds.
yet in the rush they fail to see
moon-like crescents under the tree.

the silver moon has blotted out
and light is gone as children shout;
while shadows chase the world, enhance,
and calves kick up their heels and prance.

yet then it's gone, the sun is bright
dark retreats from the growing light;
the birds begin to sing again,
cows return to the empty glen.

yet in the rush they fail to see
moon-like crescents under the tree.

glasses are gone as children play
parents prepare for endless day;
they say that all is said and done
lonely now is the golden sun.

they saw a wonder so unique—
it must have been beyond the peak;
but as doors shut, the glory grows
stunning colors and secret glows.
yes, in the rush they failed to see
moon-like crescents under the tree.

## morning's song

i don't know how dawn breaks—

sun rises so

beautifully becoming, extracting the dew.

when shadows and whispers light up in morn'

grass suddenly giggles with drops

and the rose too

clothed in gems.

that sun line creeping across the lawn,

and now it's warm, tinge of leftover frost,

the sweetness of dawn.

i wonder how morning arrives.

in one moment—snap of ginger cookie

or like the slow oozing of pudding

dripping from my spoon?

this change: evolution or transformation?

yet i see it in me too,

the way Jesus took my night, darkness,

gave me His light—

ultimate exchange

as He melted my frost into dew.

and secret solace:

dawn breaks continually

all over the world's curvature

in rays that light up the morn'.

# my prayer

as i wake this morning
this is my heart
that i could love just one person
lighten the dark

shine Jesus' truth
when both gentle and hard
and after all's over
know that He loved

Caroline Rutledge

# old lovers

thin, scrambling tresses
of vines, draped
and curled around old wood.
a blossom peering between splinters,
pale pink on dry brown—
the weather-worn bench
faded, marred by time and carved
by a knife of two lovers.
two initials with a heart
while winding vines adorn,
sweeping down like a gull.
white feathers shining in ocean wind,
salty spray.
but instead petals perfume,
scent the antique bench
where a couple once stood

sealing their love into old wood.
and a flash of spotted grey-brown,
claws on the dust,
wings flit to the abandoned scene,
a sparrow's home.
two lovers and three
little eggs.

where i sit now with One
who loved me first.

# petrichor

wet socks that cling to my feet

sticky, moist, but they won't

let go.

and it's okay

because all i want

is to dance

here.

splashing puddles and soggy grass,

raindrops on my hair;

song of the rain i hear.

the perfume of moist flowers

and soil absorbing

the coolness.

my socks cling to the mud

hold onto water,

and i just keep dancing

because the rain makes melody
only i can hear.
and maybe if i dance
someone else will hear the song—
perhaps they'll see the beauty
let their feet fly free
and get their socks wet
unabandoned.

# simple love

it's Who You are, the yearn of my soul.

so simply whole, single passion beating:

a rainstorm, where all is one thundering chord.

i'm one drop in a million

*—Your storm of Love—*

yet You know every aura

and this heart beats, wishing up

a hurricane.

wash all away, Lord, wash all away

this fray—*the sun and clouds and stars*

*a tornado of things i see and know—*

dissolved.

simple Love

blooms from a storm's erosion:

be that gust, one thundering chord

be all.

single passion beating,
simple Love.

# somehow, i met You

those eyes that hold a story,
those shoulders brushing mine—
the laughter from so far away
as You and me collide.

to stand among a hundred
or walk right through a crowd,
to be a daisy in the grass
or die without a sound.

i wonder if they see me
yet by You i am known
for even in this fleck of time
somehow my days You've grown.

i saw Your splash of light, i'm

a daisy in the grass;

and even if i'm lost, alone

my story now will last.


grow forever

                                            reaching high.

because You.

# song for my Lover

this song is for You:

love soft like spring grass,

tender sprigs appearing from glass snow,

a breeze—*Your whispers*—

cool like the morning birds sing again.

this world is dead, so dead

You breathe life:

daffodil yellow and secret wildflowers, hidden

in forest logs and damp humus;

life rests in the soil, ready to spring,

to dance.

i want to join the call,

i need to.

lungs burn from the cold, but

i smell flowers.

and i will awake to the voice of my Lover

in a new morn',

and Your mercies are new too.

glory, this spring love—

that You see me, a weed,

rename me a wildflower and make me

Your own to love.

# spring snowflakes

i saw snowflakes leaping—

newborn calves in spring, first lamb,

everything in white and green

as if winter crept off its page and jumped

into spring's tale.

the fluff of dandelions, moist

with ice,

daffodils kissed with flakes,

song of winter and spring birds colliding.

it's like an eclipse:

moon grasping sun,

two foreign beings, seeing each other for first time.


gasp.

i saw my breath

mixed with flurries

on green grass and my loose hair
kissed by sunshine
only yesterday.
a million crystals watching a gosling hatch,
smelling flowers' aroma
and mowed lawns.
and yes, the snow is leaping with the pulsing
of newborn calves' dance in tiny hooves.

it's all a dance, a hug, a song
or laughter
of something so absurd and wonderful
like the love You have for me.

Josiah Dyck

@josiah_dyck_artist

# supine

it's been so long.

forgotten hideaway i used to roam,

but i'm here again—

remembering old memories

while making new ones.

this memory is my favorite,

as i lay here, wince,

remove the branchy thorns,

and try again.

face to the sky

i hear birds and bugs, cows lowing

far away.

but my eyes

they're blurry.

am i going to cry or have i just forgotten how

to see?

it's been so long.

me writing, paper in the air above me,

blocking the sky.

i lower it, try to glimpse

twinkles of tender leaves,

colors of fall with kisses of spring,

and under the gold, colors indescribable:

like green, but yellower

or brown, but richer.

the tree bark—

true black, grey, brown

and snippets of minty moss creeping up.

it's been so long.

i wonder why.

because now i smell leaves

moist from yesterday's rain.

i see little bugs dancing,

and a piece of white fuzz

flies past without wings.

little miracles as i lay

and smile.

there's a tree with limbs broken like a ladder;

i could climb to Jesus

if only i could reach the first branch.

i wonder why i forgot

and how i can see again.

so i remember

as God gives me this new memory.

i lay, and He

lifts me higher

than i could ever go.

somehow He loves me.

# the Lamb's song

Praise—
i hear music, even whispered
like a kiss from slender lips;
quiet, secret words of praise.

Honor—
as my hair falls before my face
bowing, kneeling
embrace of soil and me,
where weddings begin,
and i see no other.

Glory—
scribbled pen strokes, a brush,
hasty paint on canvas.
but real color is all around

heart explodes, dance.

Supremacy—
hand limp, i tremble, shake
'til music all around me
battle cry, hand of mountains, heavens
song this world utters, reverent.

i join the melody, swept away:

*to Him who sits on the throne and to the Lamb*
*be praise and honor and glory and supremacy*
*forever into the ages of the ages!*

Lisa Elis

# to know

i love to know this God
Who slips honey in the heart of the grass
and it dries, sweet,
hay at my ankles, autumn perfume.
Who formed the softness of the ragweed,
lets her leaves grow in pieces
as if torn by a child's touch,
and it tickles our noses every summer.
Who breathes life and made us long for that touch;
a sister's feet against me as she slumbers,
or four paws massaging, eyes begging,
and even this, me, eyes and heart lifted
sifting through turfs of straw and hay
to see treasure.
who promised a New Earth where i can touch
Him.

i love to know this God.

# two words

i always wonder how 26 letters
make up this entire world we know.
how writers spin them like pottery wheels
to words of beauty:
like luminescence, tranquility, aura
and ones of meaning:
beginnings, satisfaction, forever.
the mixing of the two becomes glossy paint on oven-baked jars,
and yet i've found
nine letters are enough—
two words—
to capture beauty and meaning and this entire world we know.
like the beginning of a book, somehow the ending too
or like a simple clay setting perfect in beauty.
two words:

o n l y  J e s u s .

so i worship.

# when love lives on

if emotion is all that Love can be
then Love is naught.
an ember burning bright must also fade;
nothingness swallows up
'til all remains a sliver of coal,
cold and grey.

does Love too die, everlasting
star shine forevermore
eyes winking out in light of dawn?
or is it more?
living on when emotion dies,
when failure falls,
can Love defeat death,
shine bright amidst darkness?

deeper than glistening ocean waves,

reflections from silver moon rays.

for even the stars,

though hidden, continue to shine

in light of day.

# windswept silence

twirling eddies, rustling colors spin together—

tornado in cool breeze

pushing, throbbing, grabbing at my hair;

i am spun in the dance.

invisible fingers close around mine:

the wind's song, and my feet

never touch the ground.

soft drops of rain, a crystal chandelier,

breathless melody of thunder's

lightning far off—distant star.

my wet feet, hair around my shoulders,

silent gasp with windblown leaves

like the rainbow before a storm.


all stills before the drop of an acorn

glistening drops cling to every bud

watching

for the voice of the storm

to call us into the dance again.

but until then

we wait.


frozen dance floor against my toes,

the beckoning that the breeze

longs to hear.

the storm's invitation for me

to dance, to spin, to live

truly live

again

and forever.

# yet a garden amidst the desert

i'm learning to skip through the desert.

it's hard, tears blinding me,

salt on sand,

and the skipping doesn't erase the wasteland:

choking, burning.

sand bitter in my throat;

sweat trickles down my spine,

and sometimes the only shadow i see is my own.

i cry

but skip too.

there's a second set of footprints beside mine,

and Jesus, You are there.

i've never been more hurting, cried so much,

yet i've never been more loved.

this world is a desert—

You whisper *let's find My garden.*

so we do.

we traipse this arid land

where You point out the cacti flowers

or a lull in the dunes, and You promise

*there's a river beneath—*

*one day it will burst, and roses will bloom.*

You have me lift my eyes to a hundred,

so many pilgrims on this dusty road

together,

and You call them Yours,

which makes us family.

so we cry and laugh and fight and travel on.

Your garden is worth this.

but until then, You fill my canteen with spring water,

point to where dusty brown meets baby blue,

and say, *press on child.*

You give me all i need,

while pointing out the wild deer and first sprigs of green.

You make me

loved.

while sweat soaks my skin, i look forward to newness,

yet i've never been happier

than this moment with You, Jesus,

never been more in love.

You're bringing a garden:

tender orchids, trees laden with fruit and moss,

waters dancing between our feet.

there'll be coolness, tenderness forever.
You'll turn this wasteland into a garden,
i will travel on with You,
skipping through the desert.

behind the poems

## a word, a life

One of my life verses is Psalm 127:1, and it's foundational for this poem which opens the collection. Sometimes, I reword the verse and pray it like this:

*unless the Lord writes the words,*
*they labor in vain who write it.*

Ah, my desire for this entire anthology is in that verse! May my King and Father write these words. May the poems represent a tiny picture of His heart.

That's my biggest dream for every single poem. *Unless the Lord.* It's all about Him.

*roots*

## abundance

*Psalm 36:8*
*Psalm 37:11*
*Matthew 9:37-38*
*Mark 12:44*
*John 10:10*
*Ephesians 3:20*

Art by Caroline Ruth

# a glimpse

Art by Tarissa Hughes

poem based on *Revelation 21:1-5*

"Then I saw 'a new heaven and a new earth,' for the *former* heaven and the *former* earth had passed away, and the sea was no longer there. I saw, too, the holy city, the New Jerusalem, coming down out of heaven from God, prepared and ready, like a bride beautifully adorned for her husband. Then I heard a booming voice from the throne say, 'Look! The tabernacle of God is with mankind! He will tabernacle among them, and they will be peoples, yes, belonging to him, and among them will dwell God himself. He will "wipe away every tear from their eyes," and death will be no more. There will be no more mourning or wailing or anguish, for the present order of things is destined to pass away.' And the one seated on the throne said, 'Listen! I am going to make the whole creation new!' Then he added, 'Write it down, because these words are fully trustworthy and reliable.'"

# blind color

One of my favorite movies is *The Giver* because it captures the heart and awe I wrote about in this poem, the desire to truly *see.*

I'm a fast-paced, productive girl. While that's often helpful (like not procrastinating on college papers!), I've had days when I sat to write in my nightly journal, and I realized I forgot to see.

I lived with hundreds of colors around me, but it was like I was blind to them all.

I never truly saw beauty. Smelled it. Heard music. Embraced it.

If you've ever watched a black and white film (like Andy Griffith), in the middle of the movie, you forget it's black and white. I was the opposite: I forgot to see colors in this colorful world around me. Jesus changes that. He whispers, *look up and worship. I gave you this gift.*

So I challenge myself and you: stop and look.

Sometimes I deliberately praise Him for every sense: for the beauty I see, smell, hear, taste, touch. I shut my eyes and truly listen. I take time to name the different hues of colors I see.

I challenge you to slow down, be with your King, and experience the previews of Kingdom life He has slipped into our todays.

## collage called the Church

*Romans 12*

I was in our attic War Room (where we fight battles in prayer), and as I sat before the Lord, I noticed the plywood walls.

So many fragments of wood seemed pasted together with glue, and I thought of the Church, first of the Israelites whom He uniquely chose and now the rest of the world adopted in. Today, God's people are made up of individuals from almost every country, language, and culture!

He takes our broken, faulty selves and washes us clean through Jesus' blood, invites us to be a forever family in His coming Kingdom! How beautiful that is, and how much purpose it gives us, like the strength of plywood, even if made of fragmented pieces.

## freedom

*Galatians 5:13*
*Ephesians 3:12*
*2 Corinthians 3:17*
*2 Corinthians 12:9*

## heart questions

This poem reminds me of the song by Brandon Lake "Give Me Your Eyes" which has been my prayer many times.

It reminds me of passages in the Bible that speak of people who have eyes but cannot perceive (Isaiah 6:9-10), and these heart questions are my yearning to look beyond the external to the heart that God sees and knows yet still extends kindness and mercy.

# home

Fun fact: I am not a traveler.

I enjoy trips and new scenery, but my favorite place is always home.

As I sat by a roaring, North Carolina, mountain stream, I wrote this poem. It was the desire and joy of my home several states away, but it was also the desire I have for Jesus to return and bring Home to this earth.

I love to dream of His Kingdom, not in ethereal ways but as a real home. I imagine going hammocking, making friends, picking wildflowers, exploring unknown territories, learning dances, and doing all those things in His joyous presence. I'm not a traveler, I just long for Home.

That's my hope and why I wrote this poem.

# i step into

*2 Corinthians 5:7*

"(it is by faith, you see, that we live our lives, not by sight)"

*Hebrews 11*

One morning, I found a seat on the porch to sit with Jesus, and I lived this poem.

The world was utterly foggy. I couldn't see across the pasture to where our mailbox waited for the usual delivery. The trees were blotted out, the sky too.

As the cloud wrapped its chilly arms around me, it smudged all hues into a soft grey, and all I could see was the little circle of color right around me. But if I took a step, the color moved with me. I could see through the cloud but only the few feet around my own body.

It reminds me of life and how little we can see sometimes. So often, I come before Jesus with my limited vision and whisper, "oh to let my faith be sight!"

I choose to believe despite what I can't see in hopes that one day the cloud will be lifted, and I'll be Home where I can see Jesus face to face.

A song that's encouraged me while in the thick fog is "I Can See it Now" by Josiah Chad.

## it's gonna be alright

Based on the song "Alright" by Jonathan Ogden

I wrote this poem after asking myself what "faithful" means.

This poem is about faith. It's about Hosanna holding to a belief that even though she can't see something, it's undoubtably true. It's the belief that although I've done wrong against my God and King and deserve death, He provided a way through His Son dying that death for me and rising to life again so that now I have confidence that I'm forgiven and will rise after I die to inherit His Kingdom with Him! That's the faith I cling to.

In this poem, I wondered what His *faithfulness* means. God doesn't have to be full of faith because He can see it all, right?

So I simply defined "faithful" as: *worthy of belief.*

God is so trustworthy that I can put my faith in Him and know it will come to pass. Similarly, I know even as night sets (ironically I write here near midnight), the sun is shining somewhere, thus the sun is faithful to rise: it's worthy of belief. So is God.

I'll have faith even if it doesn't make sense; they might think me crazy, but this crazy faith in a King who is bringing a Kingdom is the happiest life I've ever known. I could dance through all the years in the sweetness of having faith in real-life dreams that *will* come true.

## oracles

*Psalm 119*

I wrote this poem for the moments when truth feels far away. When you read the Bible and know its promises, but they don't seem tangible. When discouragement creeps in as lies to stifle faith like tarnish on brass.

Go back to the whispers that began this adventure. The oracles that promise a Kingdom and a hope. Hold on to truth. Hold onto Jesus, and if you seek Him, He will be found. I promise. (Matthew 7:7-11)

It reminds me of Andrew Peterson's song "You'll Find Your Way."

## renewed

*Isaiah 40:31*
*Psalm 103:1-5*

Fun fact: we have few eagles where I live, so the inspiration for this poem was from the soaring of buzzards' silhouettes against the sky. How poetic would "buzzard eyes on the horizon" sound?

## shaped by the future

This is one of my favorite poems. *grin* I don't know why, but I get so excited by the dual impact in my life of what Jesus did in the past (Romans 5:6-8) and His promises for the future (Romans 8:16-25)! Both His humble, awe-inspiring death and sacrifice as well as His promise of resurrection life and living in a forever Kingdom where I am a fellow heir and am glorified with Him, they both define my life and how I dance through every single day. That reality really makes me happy and causes this girl who isn't skilled in dancing to want to skip around! *laughs*

And fun fact: the line referencing turning from a pauper to a princess always reminds me of a Veggie Tales' movie, *The Penniless Princess.*

## shattering darkness

When I lose vision of who I am and who God is in this world, a chapter I read is Job 38. To look above me and my life and imagine great wonders like the place where light dwells or the treasuries of snow and hail, it causes me to whisper praise to this God who is so beyond me. The awesome thing is that He ascribes value to me, little Hosanna who is nothing compared to the One who put the belt on Orion and guides the Great Bear with its cubs.

He looks at me and says He desires me to live in His coming Kingdom.

He says I was worth His Son's death.

I crawl into this great God's arms like a Daddy God and whisper this poem as a praise of my imagination of how grand He is.

## silence of the day

The first time I went hunting, I was surprised at how noisy the mornings are as even before the sun rises. Birds wake early and fill the sky loudly with singing and choruses!

At the same time, I've walked through summer nights where bullfrogs and crickets blast their music under the starry skies. It left me wondering if the quietest time of the day might be right at noon as animals rest in the shade and take their "siesta." (it may be equally quiet between midnight and dawn, but I'm not awake to know…)

The idea made me wonder if the world quiets because these daylight hours are our time, as beings in His image, to make our own worship to the Lord.

The birds awake the world in worship. The bugs and frogs sing lullabies to sleep. And we, in the middle get:

*to let this soul sing its starring role,*

I love that. *grin*

## something crazy

I'm not an adventurous person. I don't enjoy rollercoasters or want to travel the world or dream of breaking world records. When I climb trees, I don't go too high. I don't speed in my car (or at least not on purpose…)

Ah, but I do want to do something utterly crazy. It's the yearning bubbling in me like a scalding pot of boiling water.

I want to live a life fully surrendered to Jesus. I want to have a predetermined "yes" to any command He whispers.

Yes, I'll sell all I have and give it away. Yes, I'll move to the jungles or slums or wastelands to share His Good News. Yes, I'll sacrifice my dreams for something greater. Yes, I'll give my life and die as a martyr to be found faithful to Him.

I've grown up on missionary stories, of people who lived and died and sacrificed for Jesus, and that's what I want more than anything—to come to the end of life and know I lived it well for Him.

I'm willing to do something crazy, for You, my King. And I'm willing to live ordinary life for you too. I just ask You to live life in me.

## some things never change

As a pre-teen, I imagined how awesome of an adult I'd be (anyone else do that?).

I'd be like Katie Davis in *Kisses from Katie* and be brave to travel across the world to share Jesus. I'd be beautiful with no more acne marks, know how to fancy up my disobedient hair, and be completely comfortable in group settings. I'd get married right out of high-school, have a dozen kids, and live all my dreams. My struggles would be gone.

Then I grew up.

Growing up isn't all bad, for there's amazing blessings. I'd never imagined myself publishing books, working at a music store I love, having an incredible family and community who is seeking Jesus faithfully!

But me, little Hosanna, she still struggles.

She still gets scared, has acne, has hair that's curly only when it wants to, and prefers not to speak in a group. She still struggles.

It taught me: if I was perfect, I wouldn't need Jesus.

Today I'm an adult. I make mistakes and I'm lost without Jesus. But I love Him more than I ever have and need Him more than before.

That never changes, and I'm so happy.

## wait, dear heart

*Isaiah 55:8-13*

I sat and penned this poem during a bitterly sweet season where God took something good in my life and whispered, "will you wait on me for this so I can bring forth something even better?"

A childlike quote became my prayer:

*"Good, better, best.*
*Never let it rest*
*Until your good is better*
*And your better best."*

I learned that God's ways are higher than my own. That out of His great love, He invites me to wait to gain a treasure so much more valuable.

Today as I write with September wind pulsing my hair, I continue to wait and see the answer to that prayer. But I know His thoughts are beyond mine and His promises completely true and trustworthy.

The passage in Isaiah (which is beautifully quoted in "Sower's Song" by Andrew Peterson) was a theme for this poem. I rest, fall asleep as I wait, trustingly, for the storm clouds to roll around and bring rain to satisfy this thirsty heart in me.

## wistful gusts

One of my first memorized poems as a child was "Who Has Seen the Wind?" by Christina Rosetti, and it inspired this poem.

Since the day I heard that poem, I've imagined seeing the wind. In my poem, I keep dreaming. I imagine holding the wind too, feeling its power surge through a kite as my hands try to control it.

But sometimes, the hardest is simply hearing the wind.

We rush through the day and forget "zephyr's song." We forget to truly listen.

I'm returning to that childlike place of wonder where I really see wind, hold it, and hear it. The days that are given me are a precious commodity, and I want to use every minute as a praise for the One who created all.

## witness of twilight

I sat by a campfire with a friend, and we looked up at the stars shining in a clear sky. I whispered, "Do you ever imagine stars are like pinpricks where we can see light shining from God's throne room?"

She laughed, saying, "I'm totally a science girl, so I think of meteoroids burning in space."

Okay, so maybe it was my poetic, whimsical dreaming coming out, but I'm okay with that.

God is teaching me to love what He loves. Thus, I sit and stare at the nature He made and rejoice. I imagine how I'd write beauty in poetry. I try to capture color and texture in words. I worship.

Yet another huge part of loving what He loves is seeing people with His eyes, sitting among a crowd of individuals of so many personalities, backgrounds, weaknesses and simply loving them because they're made in His image, and He sees them as valued.

May our hearts reflect His if we're science-y and literal or poetic and dreamy. Either way, may we love what He loves and worship.

(a passage I love is Psalm 19)

thorns

## a look not taken

This is a fun story.

My brother and I decided to go on our first big road trip. It would be 12+ hours, four states, and all within three days.

We planned. I gave it to God multiple times, being a tad nervous. We packed. Then the day came, and we jumped in our little Civic and drove off!

Driving down the road, we gave the car to God and told Him we trusted Him to take care of it for us how He desired (if you've never heard of "The Pineapple Story" by Otto Koning, this is the perfect time to fix that!)

One hour later, a tow truck slammed into us (yeah, oops). When the car stopped spinning, I remember looking at my brother, and we burst out laughing.

Because the trip belonged to God and so did the car and our very lives. We weren't concerned with what happened, we were just so thankful we were in a car wreck and were both completely fine. (the next moment, I peeked in the rear-view mirror and said, "The car looks really bad," but laughing came first.)

Every step was a miracle: The car came to a stop on the side of the road with no traffic in sight. We didn't flip. No one was injured. A bystander brought us water bottles while we waited to be towed. My brother got to share Jesus with the people involved. There even was a porta potty on the side of the road right where we waited.

*Jesus was in that moment.*

I won't say we didn't have slight PTSD every time we were in a car that breaked quickly. (Yikes.) But as I got home and unpacked from the trip we had to cancel, I needed to process. This poem came out only a few hours after the accident.

It's a reminder to be alert, eyes open, to what the Lord puts before you. Like the driver who should have taken that look to see if his road was clear, I desire my eyes to be open to the hearts and souls around me. I pray, "Oh Lord, give me eyes to see!"

## apparition, i know not

The line that hits me in this poem is:

*were the colors real or is this mirage... reality*

Do you ever feel this? Sometimes the darkness is so dark that it feels like morning light is a hundred miles away.

We're living for a coming Kingdom (where Jesus is King!), but the enemy tightens his grip on this age and squeezes. He throws lies at us like fiery arrows. We're Robin Hood's Merry Men banished but waiting in this time of trouble, standing up for truth, and knowing that one day the King will reign. (not sure where stealing from the rich would fit in, so ignore that please. *laughs*)

Ahh, these days when our souls are blurred by the fog of this present evil age as the enemy attacks! May we be found pursuing the Kingdom regardless. May God's Word be a light to our feet. May we fight in prayer and in exhorting one another. May we remember that God will win the battle, and His Son will reign as King.

Let's find the real colors and claim hold to them in this mirage. He who promised is faithful. Don't lose heart.

## appomattox

In the fall hues, our family took a trip to Virginia and spent an afternoon at the historic Appomattox Court House where the treaty was signed between Lee and Grant to end the US Civil War.

This history-loving girl saw it all. From the red-brick building itself to little homes, cemeteries, and even slave quarters preserved over the years, we roamed the park. But my heart grew heavy.

At one place, we stood where the last shot was fired, soldier died on green grass. Another place we could see the exact ridge armies had poured forth from, and we also stood at the very ground where the two companies lined up to hand over their bayonets and declare peace, one cause going home defeated.

I could cry, could mourn, for a cause that shed so much blood and gained nothing. And yet the warrior spirit in me glows hot as I remembered that as the bedraggled, defeated army marched past their victors in surrender, the winning side cheered them on and received them as brothers.

That's what I saw as I visited Appomattox. I saw where blood once stained fresh soil—horrible and ugly—but as I asked Jesus where worship was, I saw that too. There was worship in that moment, in the humility of an army and the acceptance of brotherhood.

Not that there weren't problems after the war. But maybe that moment of surrender had something purposeful and good too, and that's what I want the poem to declare in victory.

## battlefront revelation

Art by Nicole ElsieRose

Artist notes: "*I wanted to focus on how the Lord wraps His everlasting arms around us and pulls us out of the darkness and into His marvelous light, where we are saved, made whole, and loved completely. I also wanted to portray the feeling of falling into His arms and the relief and healing that comes with it.*

*"These past few months, I personally have been in the place of the girl in my illustration. In this piece, I poured the truths that the Lord has been teaching me in this time of weariness and needing peace in my soul, and I placed a focus on the comfort that His Presence is a Shield around all those who take refuge in Him. It serves as a reminder to myself, and I hope for you too, that Jesus offers this relief every moment. There is no need to battle on without Him, and in fact, we cannot do it alone... we were never meant to. Jesus is just waiting for us to lean onto Him and make our home in His arms, where we truly belong, where we were always meant to dwell.*"

## beyond procellous

my definition:
*a storminess, like a tempestuous sea*

## bursting forth

*Isaiah 35*
This poem is inspired by me being the oldest girl in my family with 7 younger siblings. I used to feel like that meant I had to be perfect. I had to have things figured out, walk perfectly with the Lord, and never struggle. I didn't like if they saw me cry, and I didn't want to cause them to question anything.

But those were lies, and they couldn't be fulfilled even if I tried hard. I wasn't perfect, and I would fail. That was okay (our God is so good at forgiving!). So obviously, you can ask any of my siblings and they'd say they've seen me cry, they know I make mistakes, sometimes I can be bossy or distracted, but hopefully they'd say I ask forgiveness and love them so so much.

I've had other people comment on how I have things figured out, I must be always joyful, and I'm an amazing person to look up to; this poem is my response to all that. I laugh because without Jesus, I'm completely lost, messed up, and weak. Any good in me is from Him, and I'm okay with being open and vulnerable about the fact that yes, I still do mess up. I'm still weak. I still make mistakes in my writing, get to places late, get confused by crazy emotions, and get scared sometimes too.

But His strength is made perfect in weakness (2 Corinthians 12:9). I'm basing my life on that!

## caducous

Art by Lisa Elis

my definition:
*when something falls too early*

## condensation

Fun fact: I do most of my writing at my desk where I can see straight through a window to the outside world. In summer, there are cows grazing as ducks, chickens, and geese wander around their feet, but when the cold settles in, the pastures grow empty. In this poem, I'm sitting at that desk looking at the condensation that clings to the edges of the window as frost lines the world, and I attempt to capture that moment in simple poetry.

## dear irah,

In a Georgia hotel, I slipped through the breakfast lines and paused with a full plate and cup of juice (apple and orange mixed, of course). My introvert self looked for a place by my family to steal away to, laugh and exchange how our nights went in a comfortable seat in this room of half-asleep strangers.

Our family of twelve took up multiple tables, and we loved these mornings to chat. But somehow, another table caught my eye.

I approached the girl, a pre-teen only a few years younger than me with tanned skin and a Middle Eastern look. She had beautiful, sleek-black hair, and we chatted and ate and became friends in a few minutes.

Her name was Irah. After breakfast, we left, and I joined my family in the long drive down to Florida. As pines turned to Spanish moss, I kept thinking of Irah.

I'd never see her again. But I saw a hint of sadness, a hollow look in those dark eyes, so I sat in the bumps of our van and wrote this poem for her.

It reminds me of all the other eyes in that dining room and every place I go, the eyes that are sad or empty or worried. It reminds me to look beyond myself, take a table with a stranger, and love them.

And it reminds me that without Jesus, life is oh, so shallow. He's my reason for joy and life! And may we love that person before us, truly listen, and really get to know a person and love them like He does.

## dear one

I can't read this one without the song "Don't You Give Up on Me" by Brandon Lake coming to mind.

## eternity's glow

This poem stems on a thought: the stars are *always* shining.

Even when the sun is startlingly bright and the sky doused in blueness so thick you can't see the stars. Even when clouds blot them out. Even when the night is darkest.

The stars are always shining.

It reminds me to never give up hope.

Jesus has promised to return and bring His Kingdom and restore this broken earth. He has promised a land of abundance, where roses burst into bloom in the desert and waters flow in the wilderness (Isaiah 35). He will be King, and we will be His children, reigning with Him! The dead will experience resurrection life, and joy will be forever! I dig through the Bible, clinging to that hope and dreaming of it with girlish joy!

*because it will become Reality.*

  *proceeds to fangirl over how awesome God is*
  ("When Love Lives On" is another poem with similar imagery of the stars! If you can't tell, I'm one of those girls who sits under the night sky and could lay for hours watching. *wink*)

## extramundane

  my definition:
  *relating to something beyond what we can see in this present earth and time*

## exposed

  This poem reminds me of the song "Known" by Tauren Wells. I'm blown away by the fact that God knows all of me yet loves me anyway and nothing can separate me from that love (Romans 8:31-39)!
  I don't know who first wrote this poem, but it's fitting:

  *"He knows, He loves, He cares; nothing this truth can dim. He gives His very best to those, who leave the choice with Him."*

## first frost

  I used to dislike autumn. Everyone else raved about pumpkin and cinnamon, but I saw frost suffocating summer flowers and turning the world to a grey stillness.
  One autumn evening while a friend and I walked to our cars after a busy workday, she said something simple. She told me of a time she felt

the same sadness when fall came, but someone challenged her to look for the beauty in autumn.

So I did.

I've since fallen in love with autumn. I'm the silly girl who raves about pumpkin spice and campfires and finally wearing sweaters again!

But life has other things like this, situations that are hard. There're days I wake in bed and have to push off lies like stifling blankets.

Something I've learned to whisper is Psalm 118:24 which I believe describes the days of the Lord... the day He first came as a suffering Servant and the Day He comes again as a victorious King. I bank my joy and my upcoming 24 hours on that, thus I rejoice and am glad!

My favorite lines from the poem:

> *today's the best day of my life*
> *because Jesus*
> *is here, in me*

... even in frost.

## goodbye

To be honest, I don't remember what inspired this poem, and I even pondered slipping it out of the collection altogether.

But I'm letting its ink bleed onto the paper because it captures a pain we all feel. It draws me back to a time I performed in the theatrical version of *Anne of Green Gables*, and for the last showcase, the director told us "Carpe diem: seize the day."

As we acted out the show, I did just that. I savored every line, every color, every actor and actress around me. As Mattie—a girl version of Matthew Cuthbert—I loved Anne fully and died a beautiful death. *insert sobs*

I seized that moment and lived it fully. When it was done, I could cry a bucket of tears, but I think back with joy that I completely embraced that moment.

So as we live life, may we also "carpe diem."

Goodbyes are sad. They hurt.

But may we learn to embrace the "hello"s and every single moment in between so that those "goodbye"s hurt terribly just because we were willing to risk loving even if it hurt.

# higher vision

As a poet, when I see something beautiful, I try to come up with words to describe it, yet so often it's beyond me. I glimpse a shade of color that cannot be contained in a few adjectives. I view a cloud that has texture, shape, emotion beyond what 26 letters can tell. My only explanation: God is amazing and so beyond me.

I keep trying, and I expect I'll do that all my life.

This poem gives you the opposite challenge: take my simple words and try to expand your mind and see the beauty of the fullness I based this poem on.

Another theme of this poem that I love can be found correlating with this passage:

*John 12:24-26*

"Amen, amen, I solemnly tell you this: Unless a grain of wheat, by being sown into the ground, 'dies,' as it were, it remains only a single seed. If it dies, however, then it produces what? A large harvest. If someone is unwilling to let go of his life, he will surely lose it. If someone is prepared to give up his life in this world, however, it is unto life in the age to come that he will keep it. If someone wants to serve me, he must with me continue on as a disciple, so that wherever I am, at that same place my servant, too, himself will be. If someone serves me, the Father will honor him."

# i shall not want

*John 11:26*
*Isaiah 1:18*

If you've read my fantasy novel *The Torch Keepers,* this is a poem right out of the heart of that story.

It's a picture of someone broken who is forgiven. Someone marred who is cleaned.

It's Kadira finding her blood-stained hands washed in the mountain stream as Gamma says she's forgiven and adopts her back into the family because of Father's sacrifice.

And it's a reminder that Jesus offers life, forgiveness, and mercy.

For me personally, when I'm burdened or feel like I've messed up, I walk into the wooded clearing by our home. There, I speak every worry out loud to Jesus and whisper, "I give these all to you." Wind pulses the air. I "give it to the Lord in prayer" as the hymn says and walk back to my home rejuvenated by the forgiveness He offers me as His daughter.

He is so good to forgive us and wash our hands clean!

## it won't be too long now

This poem is based on the song "See You in a Little While" by Steven Curtis Chapman. Unbeknownst to me while writing it, only five days later, I'd be saying the same broken "goodbye" to my little niece who was born prematurely.

I never got to hold lil' Everly Praise. I never got to kiss her, hug her, take her into the sunshine and show her how the geese honk so loudly, and the cows want to lick her hand through the fence.

But I'll see her in a little while, and it won't be too long now.

I didn't see her frail, earthly body, but I will see her when her body is resurrected on that Day as the little lady God made her to be. I'll grab her tiny fingers and dance with her in Jesus' sweet presence. We'll share life—but not this broken one marred with sickness and thorns and tears— life unexplainably beautiful and perfect and good.

I'll miss her, cry, but ah, Evie, I'll see you then.

## life's colliding colors

I'm an old-fashioned girl who writes snail mail, types on a typewriter, and would totally use a telephone booth or jump on my horse and buggy.

And yet life moves on. Those gems of memories fade. I used to wonder why God put me in the 21st century instead of living in a log cabin beside Laura Ingalls.

Things die though, just like we will, but it doesn't end morbidly there. The poem describes white cheeks and the pallor of death, but my favorite line:

*when resurrection's in her eyes*

One day that'll be me, and I'm giddily excited!

A key truth for those following King Jesus is that He was the firstborn from the dead (Colossians 1:18), which means He was the first one who got to experience resurrection, and we get to be next! I just get this picture of a girl gone from home for too long, and she throws open the door and rushes in with light in her eyes and the hugest smile as she gasps for breath declaring, "I'm home!"

This body of Hosanna's will die one day, but it will be raised once again. I'm gonna be ready to run to Jesus in the Kingdom He creates and say the same words with pink in my flushed cheeks, "I'm home!"

Sometimes the old dies for something better to rise. But it's totally okay to be giddy over typewriters. *wink*

## live

I challenge you, dear reader:
> to pause your reading
> to look up
> to live.

To soak in the color and life and purpose around you. To see the hearts and souls beating in every person. To whisper a prayer for help and find God in the world around you.

He is there, and He desires us to seek Him.

*live.*

## lost one

This poem is me, lost and inept without Jesus.

This poem is God reaching out tenderly as a Father and calling to His lost children. It's the father of the prodigal throwing a party when his wayward child comes home.

And it's my prayer for people I hurt for, people who are lost and running from a finish line and a prize that's worth more than this world itself. I pray this for every soul, that they'd see the treasure of Jesus and of how losing themselves to find Him is a joy unspeakable.

*give up, please*
*give in.*

# oceanicity

This was the first free-verse poem I ever wrote (do you see any change from this one to one of my last ones written, "Happiness"?).

I was seventeen and taking my first on-campus college class. In any spare moment, I wrote poetry.

As I crafted this, I pictured myself standing on the edge of the ocean with the salty wind throwing back my hair. And there, despite my mistakes, flaws, and attempts to live life in my own strength, I hear Jesus calling.

He knows my name. That act of Him pursuing me has altered my life, and this poem is a picture of that invitation to let go, come to Him, and let oneself be changed.

# one month later

One year in October, the roses were in full bloom, red-pink blossoms. The same time, my little brother's best friend, Michael, finished his race and went to be with Jesus at a young age.

It was the hardest October we ever had. There were tears—so many tears—and memories we missed. When we gathered to worship, we could barely sing because of the crying. Yet it was a beautiful October too, beautiful because Michael's cancer and pain were gone, he was with Jesus, and we had that amazing hope!

A month later, the first snow came. How unique to see those still blushing rose petals edged with something so foreign as snow. I slipped out my camera to capture that moment, and it reminded me of only four weeks prior, before death came, before winter made the petals wilt.

And it reminded me that spring would come. In winter, the roses would be pruned, and they'd retreat into the frozen soil. We would cry, miss our young friend.

But ahh, spring! To know the roses will bloom once again, and one day Jesus will return to resurrect His children and give them a New Earth in incorruption! The curse will be removed, and all will be made new. We'll dance in His presence with Michael.

That's the hope in the silent tears of this poem.


## only a candle


*Revelation 2:10*

"…Remain faithful even to the point of death, and I will give you the victor's crown of life."
out of bounds


Art by Caroline Ruth


Psalm 103:11-12


Fun Fact: my 13-year-old brother and I chatted one day about how much we like the word "fjords" from reading stories of Vikings (such as books by Lois Walfrid Johnson) and how poetic it sounds, so I modified this poem to include the word just for fun. Writers can do that. *wink*

This poem is partly based off childhood memories of playing hide-and-go-seek in the entire house with the lights off. (like if the power went out... that was so. much. fun!)


## overthrown


This poem merges my thrill for medieval things, love of stories, and the hope of Jesus' coming Kingdom in one piece. It's simply a snippet of a tale, leaving the rest of the details to the reader's imagination. It's your turn to dream it up. *wink*

But it's also the simple desire of my own heart. As I've fallen in love with Jesus and gotten to know Him more and more, there truly is no sacrifice too great to make for Him. He lives life with me, and I desire Him more than anything. It's something I aspire to, pray for, and I need Him to grow me so much. Yet I seek to be the humble maiden in the story, giving up all for a King's cause if He so asks because of the joy of His forgiveness through the cross, His future hope, and the promise that He is in today with me.

# potsherd

my definition:
*a piece of broken pottery*

This poem came from my childhood years. Little Hosanna roamed the creeks and woods with my brothers and neighbor friends, pretending to be Native Americans or escaping from a mean orphanage lady.

But when we wandered the creeks, my eyes were alert for chipped pieces of pottery. One piece with rich, purple stripes was a prized possession as well as an almost lavender-blue one with triangle patterns I was sure belonged to a Native American tribe once. There was also a dark, brown one with flowers.

My siblings put their special rocks and finds in their "museums." And I'm just reminded that even in those little moments, God was loving me, leading me to find those treasures that were so important to tiny me.

# sand table

Instead of a story, I have a picture with this poem.

I picture my little sisters as summer sun pours down on their chocolate-brown hair and sweat sticks to their skin. But they laugh by the porch steps as their hands float tiny boats and make sandcastles in the sand table. Half of the table has sand, the other half water, but it somehow ends up with both sides being dark, swampy ponds. They come inside with dirty sand all over their hands, feet, hair, and faces, ready to turn the bathtub brown too.

But the picture reminds me that even these messy pictures in life have a beauty. I want to stop and see them. Thus, I attempted to describe it here.

## supercilious

my definition:
*an ugly haughtiness or pride*

## the distance

This poem reminds me of *Pilgrim's Progress* by John Bunyan. In one scene, Christian walks on the path to the Celestial City, and he's told to set his eyes on a shining light and that if his gaze remains on it, he'll find his way. But for a moment, he looks away and runs into a muddy situation (literally).

Whatever is going on in your life today, friend, I pray you look above it to that light. May you seek Jesus and want Him more than anything else, because He will be found (Jeremiah 29:13).

You are being loved.

## the secret of the thinking tree

I wrote this poem for a poetry contest (and promptly lost), but I still savor the memory, sitting on a large, flat rock that jutted out of the creekbed in a wooded thicket. So much green surrounded me along with the laughing of the water in my ears. I had a title and needed a poem to accompany it.

So I penned what I love: that God takes all of me and invites me into His very near presence. That because of Jesus' sacrifice for me, I get to exchange my messy, faulty life for His perfect one, and I am completely forgiven. What joy that He "fixes broken me"!

(It reminds me of the song "No One Ever Cared for Me Like Jesus" by Steffany Gretzinger!)

Fun fact: as I sat writing, a red fox leaped across the creek right before me! That made my day!


## this celebration

I wrote this poem after a good friend died (read "One Month Later"). And for anyone who celebrates a holiday or birthday or anniversary where that apron is hanging empty or the bowl is left unattended, this poem is for you.

I'm so sorry. I wish I could squeeze you in a bear hug. But all I can do is pray this for you, and I do. Right where you are, Friend. I love you and pray this truth wraps its arms around you today:

> *it'll be okay*
> *one day*
> *when Jesus comes home.*

And I whisper too:
"Maranatha. Come home, Lord Jesus."


## under the crimson roses

Art by Brooklyne Elysse


## voices, those voices

This is one of my most heart-felt, vulnerable poems. Because sometimes I feel like that. People look at me and think I'm a "hero," someone they respect or look up to.

But oh, this soul is utterly empty and ugly without Jesus. Without

Him, I'd have no reason for life. I'd be angry, scared, crawling into my little, safe place to hide from the world. Without Jesus, I'd be completely lost and without hope.

He's the only reason there's any good in me.

So when I felt the lies and emptiness creeping in, I wrote these raw words. But I didn't stop there. In the end, you see the speaker crawling to her feet and trying to dance.

That's me. In my brokenness, I open my arms and let Him embrace me and teach my feet to dance. He knows me completely yet loves anyway.

I'm not afraid to be broken before Him. And I'm not a "hero." I'm just a girl who gives her faulty self to Jesus' hands and whispers, "Use me. I love You and give myself to You."

He does the rest.

*blossoms*

## airplanes on the clouds

I'm in love with God, and it makes me yearn to praise Him… but lately, I've wondered what that looks like. I want to offer something great, meaningful, to this God I love who somehow loves me too and has forgiven me completely, but I sit here with empty hands, nothing worthy of His greatness.

I curled up and read Psalm 50, and God asks for a few things:
*thanksgiving. praise. to call up on Him and glorify Him.*

So today as I sat with a baby in my arms and the toddler grabbing me a paper flaking with dry paint, I wrote this poem of thanksgiving and praise.

May every day be that.

## all in the open

I love that feeling of a storm brewing, where the wind has force. This poem allows me to smell that storm on the air and the emotion billowing up where I know in this power, God is here.

Yet it fades quickly to a still, summery night when I peer past blaring porch lights to find the stars and un-twinkling planets in the evening sky.

So many times of day, seasons in life, and yet I'm surrounded by the all-consuming love of my relationship with God. It changes everything. I'm reminded of Jeremiah 29:13 that as His people in exile simply had to seek Him, I also want to look for God because He desires to be found. He hides all in the open.

Read also Matthew 7:7!

## asunder

Art by Tarissa Hughes

This poem describes a day that wind billowed across summer-y seedheads in an open field where cows roamed. My eyes feasted as spores and pollen sparkled like ocean mist, and in this moment, I worshipped.

## bubble

One of my favorite things is taking time to study something beautiful, and it could be as simple as staring at a tree's bark to see the kaleidoscope of colors in the moss and wood. In this poem, I attempted to describe the amazing beauty in a single bubble.

Growing up, it was a common thing to grab a bottle of bubble-juice (is that the right name for it?) and sit on the sun-bathed porch to create art. It took one blower, and all the siblings raced to pop them or beg for their turn to blow!

When I wrote this poem, I took time to look beyond the running, popping, laughing, and I watched a bubble escape the eager hands and lift to the skies. No one else saw it, lost in the expanse, no eyes save mine.

This poem describes that moment of finding something little and seeing beauty in it.

## butterfly tendrils

Art by Treasure Happy

When inviting creators to join the team, I really wanted to include young artists; thus, how fun when Treasure joined! She drew this picture, and as I asked what the person-shaped cloud was, she smiled (which she does a lot). "Sometimes you see a cloud that just looks like a person," she said.

So enjoy this happy, butterfly drawing by a beautiful artist!

## cascade higher

Art by Brooklyne Elysse

This poem was written from a picture writing prompt of a staircase climbing up into an open, castle-like balcony, and Brooklyne captured that image beautifully!

## crisp world

When my siblings and I were little, we played a game. As we colored pictures, we imagined every shape we colored came alive while the rest was still frozen in sleep. So we giggled as an arm "popped" to life with no body or there were eyeballs with no face.

As I'm older, I read this poem in a more serious light. *wink* I see the way my love for Jesus spurs me to use my gifts of writing passionately, and I imagine that here for every warrior creator soul—creating beauty out of an overflow of love for Him.

## dear new month

Beginnings are my favorite. At the start of every new week or month, I find myself dreaming of fun upcoming events, of writing projects to explore, and of simple moments at home where I'll get to rest with Jesus. I'm a dreamer, and beginnings are my invitation to make goals and imagine the possible adventures!

This poem was written at the dawn of an autumn month. As I wrote, I imagined what God would do in the upcoming thirty-ish days. I imagined the moments of joys and victories but also the tears, and in it, I whispered what my desire was for every single moment:

*only to know i am Yours*

Today as I write, it's the end of a month, and that's still my desire. I'll make goals and dreams, but as seasons and days pass, my ultimate focus is to know I am His. May this new month help me know that intimately a little bit more.

## fern

I could sit in the woods for hours and just look. Thus, this poem was birthed. It draws me back to quiet moments watching ferns go from curling, baby plants to straightening their leaves as mature vegetation and eventually producing spores for future greenery to overtake the forest. But it also stirs this soul to consider how God could use my little life—if surrendered to Him—to make a tiny difference like how one fern covered with spores started an entire forest.

# fire and ice

This poem was written one early morning in winter when the unmatched brightness of the snow was dazzled by a sunrise's color. The way the two married in blinding light was a moment to be savored. I wrote the poem paralleling that description with the unity of two lovers, but personally it reminds me of how complete I am with Jesus.

# fire flies

I remember a summer night when I slipped onto the porch and just looked.

Nights gets so busy with meals to eat, dishes to wash, then farm chores needing to be done, but for one moment, I stopped all that and lifted my eyes, breathed in cool, evening air, and sat with Jesus.

I'd never seen anything like it.

Growing up, I saw lightning bugs I tried to capture in my small hands and hide in a jar to become *mine*. But this time, I stared.

The fireflies blinked in syncopated rhythm. It was like a lightning show, flashing from one side of the yard to the other. It was a pattern—gentle, repeating. Soft yellows in the nighttime sky. It was magical, captivating, and I couldn't tear my eyes away.

Flashing. Dancing. Shining.

Part of me wanted to run into the fireflies and dance, become part of that beautiful act of worship to God. But instead, I watched their praise, hardly breathing.

And as I slipped back inside that night with this poem, I hoped my own life was a tiny act of worship, like how one single firefly simply creates light as it was made to do, and it turns into something greater than itself.

# flocks of beauties

I saw this moment one day, dozens of goldfinches alighting on the puffy seeds of dandelions and pecking them off, and I simply had to write it.

Oddly, this title always makes me think of violet phlox (pronounced like "flocks"), which are my favorite wildflowers. Maybe I should consider renaming it?

## goodnight, dreams

I have four sisters, and we share a room. Even though we all have our own beds, the little girls end up crawling in our blankets and begging, "Can I lay on your arm?"

So we snuggle. And talk. There are late-night stories, games we make up, and chats from silly things we did that day to serious questions about eternity.

When we were little, we'd whisper "good night," everyone else repeated it, then we would try to sleep. But if you ever wondered if you were the last one awake, you'd simply give another "good night," and find out you weren't alone in the darkness. Sometimes, there were a dozen "good night"s in a row, I'm sure!

As we grow older and fall into bed exhausted with later hours, these childhood memories are still special. And I'm always going to be thankful for the hours shared with sisters in bed when secrets come out, games and giggles are shared, and we say "good night" a hundred times.

## happiness

*Psalm 16:11*
*Psalm 19:1-4*
*Psalm 50:6*
*Romans 1:20*

This was the second to last poem written for the anthology, and it began with the idea that God is a happy God.

I'd never worded it that way. Yes, God gives joy, and yes, He is proud of His children and loves them. But He is also a happy God. In His very presence is fullness of joy, and how could that come from anything less than the God who created all joy and from whom it overflows?

My mom had the honor of picking the theme for this poem, and she laughed as she made her suggestion. She reminisced, "Sometimes when we gather to pray, I come up with childish thoughts... Instead of all the serious things to pray, I think of how God created zebras and giraffes and elephants—all sorts of funny, happy things—and I just want to thank Him for that!"

That's the heart of this poem. The wonder that we have a relationship with our Father in heaven who created a world so full of happiness because He is a God of happiness. And we get to be His kids!

## i inhale

This poem is based off several songs I've prayed while singing simply, "may every breath I take be worship!" Oh make this true of me, my King!

One such song is "Shout to the Lord." *insert heart emojis*

## love spell

This poem tries to capture the tenderness yet storm-like power of being in love with God. It's truly the sweetest thing to be loved by Jesus and belong to Him, and yet it's a love that transforms one's life to live differently and see the entire world around them in a completely new way. It doesn't settle for "mediocre" but purges us to become holy as He is holy.

I hope it challenges me and every reader to soul search if they've witnessed this sweetness. If not, I hope it brings a delight that there's so much more abundance available than they've ever imagined. And if we read with His love resonating in our soul, may we dance in the same love spell.

## moon-like crescents

In August 2017, my family stood out in the noon sun as we watched a solar eclipse. With plastic glasses or cardboard boxes with mirrors taped inside, we used special tools to see the event while protecting our eyes.

Shivers ran up my arms as—at the brightest time of day—the world grew shadowed. Nightlights flashed on. An ashy greyness covered the earth as the moon crossed the sun's path, and we saw half the sun disappear from the sky.

Somehow, the marred globe changed even the shadows of the trees. On the ground, I saw hundreds of moon-like crescents spotting the earth. And as we laughed and watched the event, I wondered if anyone else saw those flittering shadows.

## morning's song

God gave me a love for studying the Bible, and it feels extra sweet when I do it in a special place and laughingly call it our "date." In autumn, that happens to be on our porch with a fuzzy bathrobe wrapped around me as I watch leaves change every morning and see the sunrise sneak across the lawn.

There's the moment before—when the world is grey and sleepy—then sun peeks on the tops of trees. Slowly, I watch it consume the shadow of the house above my head, then sun rises, pierces my eyes and falls to light up the rose bushes with reflecting dew drops or frost that turns into like-dew wetness. It's almost magical. I still can't decide if the morning awakes slowly—evolution—or if the way it shatters the fog is quick and abrupt—transformation—because it sweeps me up in the magic. But it's the best place to be when I sit with Jesus in prayer, study, memorization, and praise!

What encourages me is that I didn't always savor these moments. I didn't love studying the Bible, so I simply asked Him to give me that love. And now every morning I can, I wiggle my way onto the porch and sit in His presence to live this poem. It's my song!

## my prayer

Fun fact: this is the shortest poem in the collection!

## old lovers

Art by Caroline Ruth

And a fun fact... while writing this, I needed to include two initials for the lovers to carve into the tree. I picked "C" and "M" because those are my parents' initials! Mama said she should print Caroline's lovely picture and hang it on our wall. *heart eyes*

## petrichor

my definition:
*the scent of fresh rain on soil after a season of lengthy dryness*

## simple love

I don't know how to describe this poem except it's my heart's prayer of overflowing love to Jesus. He's the One I love more than anything, and it's so so sweet to be loved by Him!

As I wrote, I pictured myself in a storm, arms wide as I danced in His rain of love. It was like I was a single drop, nothing to be noticed in and of myself, yet His love surrounded me in a gale, and I begged it to roar forever.

It's a similar heart to my poem "Love Spell" while the message relates also with "Song for My Lover", because it's all about Jesus, and I love Him, and that's the entire reason I live life or write any of these poems.

A favorite song that captures a similar emotion is "Laid Down Lover" by Jonathan Ogden.

## somehow, i met You

I'm one of those introverts who loves strangers (not sure how God did that…). When I first wrote this poem, that was the heart in it. When I stand in a crowd, I can't help but look at so many unknown faces, daisies in the grass, and I feel helpless. My heart yearns to know people, to discover their stories, to offer the empty eyes a wholeness in Jesus. I want to grab every person and love them, make a difference in this world.

I'm the same way. In a world of billions of people, this girl is a daisy in the grass. Just one little flower.

Sometimes I'm scared that someone will see all of me—see the brokenness and mistakes and doubts—and they'll give up on me. That they'll kneel to see the daisy and spot the mars on white petals, the weakness of the stem, and they'll look for another. It's a real fear.

Yet somehow, Jesus sees me and He knows *all of me*. He sees you too. And He chooses to love anyway. He pours himself out and gives all He has out of a great love for us marred, wilting daisies. That changes everything.

(and it reminds me of the assuring promises in Matthew 6:28-30!)

## song for my Lover

I wasn't always in love with Jesus.

I remember being a pre-teen and sitting with Mama in tears as I told her how scared I was of hell. I wanted—I needed—Jesus to save me. But it felt wrong to seek Him just for what He could do for me.

She smiled. "Hosanna," she said, "it's okay to start there. Once you get to know Jesus more, you'll love Him just for who He is."

I grew older and dove into reading the Bible, spending time with Jesus, talking with Him as a friend, memorizing His Word, and living life with Him. He surrounded me with sisters in Jesus who desired His presence.

And one day, I realized Mama was right.

I fell deep in love with Jesus, and nothing was more important than my Lover.

I still joy in what He gives me! For today, He supplies all I need for life and godliness. For eternity, He is making a New Earth for me to live in, perfect and unmarred, where I can be with Him and will be rewarded for my works on earth!

But also, I love Jesus just because of Him. He is my Best Friend. He is my Comforter. He is everything to me.

And thus this poem was created.

## spring snowflakes

I live in a state that's not quite northern but not southern either. Similarly, this is a poem based off the mixing of seasons that happens often in my confused part of America, as one day we'll have sunshine and warmth while the next turns icy with snowflakes. *happy shrugs* It's a daily wondering of how to dress, and I savor it because sometimes we get white Christmases and other times soak in the 70°s!

*of something so absurd and wonderful*
*like the love You have for me.*

## supine

my definition:
*to lay on one's back with their face lifted to the sky*

Art by Josiah Dyck

Jesus is a friend.

I remember writing this poem in a favorite spot in the woods where I used to go to be with Him. It had been so long. I'd nearly forgotten the joy and friendship and unity of being with Him in that special place.

So I went back.

And He was waiting.

## the Lamb's song

based on Revelation 5:13

(and it reminds me of a favorite song "Is He Worthy" by Andrew Peterson)

## to know

Art by Lisa Elis

## two words

This is one of my favorite poems and describes my entire heart as a writer:

*only Jesus.*

*insert all the heart emojis*

## when love lives on

*Jeremiah 31:35-37*

*Romans 8:31-39*

"In view of these things, what can we say? If God is for us, who can be against us? He who spared not even his own Son, but gave him over to death, rather, in place of us all—how in the world will he not also grant us, along with him, every other free and gracious gift? Who will bring accusation against those whom God has chosen, when God himself is the one who acquits us and sets us free? Who will succeed in condemning us, when the Messiah himself is the one who died—and even more than that, who was raised to life—for us, who also is at the right hand of God, who also continually appeals to God on our behalf? Who will separate us from the Messiah's love? Will trials or pressures or persecution or hunger or destitution or danger or sword? As it is written:

'Because of our loyalty to you we are made to face death continually; we are regarded as sheep to be slaughtered.'

No, amidst all these things we are more than victorious through the one who showed love to us. Indeed, I am convinced that not even death or life, or angels or spiritual rulers, or things present or things to come, or powers in the heights above or powers in the depths below, or anything else in all creation, will be able to separate us from the love of God that is ours in union with Messiah Jesus our Lord."

## windswept silence

Fun Fact: I'm a girl who sees a brewing storm and runs to the porch to embrace the wind pulsing my body. And if it's a rainstorm, I'm gonna grab my umbrella and be in it. Or even better, I might get a bucket of soapy water, find some eager siblings, and make it an occasion to wash our cars for free!

Yet sometimes the storms stop, and there's a beautiful calmness for a moment before it comes again to dance. Creation freezes.

And that's this poem.

## yet a garden amidst the desert

(inspired in part by the song by Josiah Chad "Travel On.")

This is the end of this anthology and the fourth-to-last poem written for the collection, so I counted the poems and had a contest of who could guess the number written. The winner was my sweet friend Rayne, and she gave me the theme of this poem. But God was already preparing my heart for this piece.

The poem is a theme of dryness and pain but with hope just around the corner, and Jesus so close one could grab His hand and walk right with Him. It's where I am in life.

This summer, I fell so in love with Jesus. I've followed Him for years, but there's this precious trust and confidence in my relationship with Him. There's nothing more wonderful than knowing Jesus.

But when my heart got to dreaming and longing for something, He stopped and asked if I could give it up for now. He had something better in the waiting (like the poem "Wait, Dear Heart").

I didn't hesitate because I love Jesus more than anything in this world. But it does hurt. This season has been hard. I've cried and seen people around me struggle so much. It's like we're walking through a desert. This age of waiting for Jesus' return is a desert.

But I have confidence: Jesus is coming back to set up His Kingdom (like a garden!) and take away all this pain. Nothing can separate us from the love of God. If we're in Jesus, we are completely forgiven and washed clean of every wrong. This life is purposeful and beautiful and so full of Hope.

I'm skipping through the desert with tears.

If these poems tell you anything, may it be this: travel on, Friend.

The prize is so worth it. Don't ever stop pursuing Jesus.

meet the warrior creators

*Brooklyne Elysse*

*"Under the Crimson Roses" + "Cascade Higher"*

*Brooklyne is a college student who is striving to live the life that God has planned for her. As an entrepreneur, she runs Winds of Faith Co., a small business selling goats milk soap, macramé, sticker designs, and other creative products. Brooklyne is passionate about faith, fitness, and farm life. She is a firm believer that God is good all the time, laughing is more contagious than yawning, and dogs are a girl's best friend.*

Fun Fact: Her love for art first came from drawing in coloring books as a child!

Instagram:  @brooklyne_elysse  @windsoffaithco
Facebook:  Brooklyne Elysse    Winds of Faith Co.

_Caroline Rutledge_

_"Abundance" + "Out of Bounds" + "Old Lovers"_

_Caroline is a beauty-creator to the core, and her fingers thrive when holding a pencil, paintbrush, or doing latte art. She spreads color and enlivens every bare chalkboard, wants to turn empty walls into vibrant murals, and her school papers were lined with the happiest doodles. Her goal is to make things that remind her of the beautiful splendor of creation. She also loves her family like crazy and fills her room with plants._

Fun Fact: Her dream as an artist is to see her work make someone happy!

Instagram: @ruthie_anne

*Josiah Chad*

*Cover Designer*

*Josiah's one aim is to bear much fruit for Jesus. Thus, he seeks to do that wherever he goes, such as in his garden full of fruit trees, vegetables, and berries. He loves spreading the news of the coming Kingdom in designing, filmmaking, song-writing, and enjoying hard work. Worshipping is his favorite, and he loves moments spent with his family. He wants every moment to be preparing for Jesus' coming Kingdom and absolutely can't wait!*

Fun Fact: One of his dreams to do on the New Earth is to raise a food forest while trimming trees. It's gonna be awesome to do that with Jesus!

YouTube:   Josiah Chad

_Josiah Dyck_

_"Supine"_

_Josiah is a Canadian self-taught artist inspired by anime and has drawn for the last two years. When not working on his next piece, you'll find him doing things like writing, gaming, spending time with his family and friends, listening to soundtracks, and just enjoying the life God has given him._

Fun Fact: His favorite colors are greens of all shades as well as the color of the sea when the water is bright and clear, such as in the Caribbean.

Instagram:   @josiah_dyck_artist
_josiahdyckauthor.wordpress.com_

*Lisa Elis*

"Caducous" + "To Know"

*Lisa lives in Canada, chasing words and art, both as work and hobby. When not staring at a computer screen, she's making coffee, taking care of plants, or listening to podcasts.*

Fun Fact: Her dream as an artist is to create full, sellable compositions that are not just pretty but hide meaning and metaphors and meditations on life, the way some artists' songs are all part of a storyline.

*lisellie.carrd.co*

*Nicole ElsieRose*

*Nicole ElsieRose is a Warrior Princess of the Lord, wearing her crown and wielding her sword of soul-woven stories—whether that be through novels, illustrations, or songs—to battle against evil... in simpler words, she is a daughter of God, doing all that she can to let her light shine in a world full of darkness.*

Fun Fact: The first artwork she remembers creating was stapling together paper as a child, writing a story on it, and illustrating! Her first story was about a dog and cat who had to learn to get along.

Instagram: @city_on_a_hill_storyteller_

*Praise Evangeline*

*Cover Illustrator and Interior Designs*

*Praise Evangeline is a left-handed girl on mission to live in Jesus'
joy and throw it all around the world. She loves expressing it in
piano worship, on a sewing machine, and while laughing freely
and hugging fiercely. Her favorite place is anywhere she can have
baby snuggles, as she dreams of being a certified doula. She enjoys
dabbling in art and loves being in the sunshine on her farm with
her big family, continually joying!*

Fun Fact: Praise has a passion for memorizing scripture and loves
hosting monthly challenges with friends and family, thoroughly
believing everyone has the superpower of memorization.

_Tarissa Hughes_

*"Asunder" + "A Glimpse"*

*Tarissa Hughes is a lover of art, usually happiest when found creating. She finds relaxation in drawing, painting, and sewing, and she dreams of seeing her artwork in someone else's home and knowing they enjoy it.*

Fun Fact: The first drawing she remembers creating was with giant crayons as she drew very pointed, snow-capped mountains with a rising sun.

Instagram: @redesignedwardrobe

*Treasure Happy*

"*Butterfly Tendrils*"

*Treasure Happy is a young artist who happily lives life with Jesus. She has a constant smile as she dances ballet, does flips around the house, dreams of being a painter, serves everyone around her, and loves math. She loves spending time with her siblings and creating in the kitchen, and if you find her at the barn, she's cuddling her cat, Poppy.*

Fun Fact: Treasure is the 9th born child in her family and loves it!

# meet hosanna emily

*Hosanna is a warrior poet: a warrior because God is her Father (which makes her a princess) and she lives fighting to be faithful for the day His Kingdom will come and a poet because she loves beautiful words.*

*Thus, she fills her journal with poetry, her blog with urges to live for Jesus, and then she writes books on top of that.*

*On a normal day, you may find her homemaking on the family farm, going on long walks, singing worship, cooking healthy food, randomly dancing the Virginia Reel, and enjoying life with her family of more than a dozen amazing people + her church family of even more.*

Fun Fact: Hosanna was blessed to have three of her siblings join her in this poetry anthology as artists! See if you can find which creators they are.

hosannaemily.com
havingaheartlikehis.blogspot.com
Instagram: @hosanna.emily

other books by hosanna emily:


The Mystery of the Midnight Trespasser
*a chapter book of riveting mystery and the*
*faithfulness of family and friendships*


The Torch Keepers
&
The Way of the King
*an allegorical fantasy duology of epic adventures, arid deserts,*
*and combating kingdoms forcing hearts to choose their side*


The Tale of Honey Waters Farm
*a chapter book of farm fun and lively adventures that point to a*
*deeper truth*


you only live twice
*a poetry collection of Holy Week and Easter; poems of the budding*
*hope of spring as resurrection blooms for the follower of Jesus*

*and now may you and i live for the Kingdom,*
*dear Warrior Creator,*
*may we fight with eyes on the King*
*for His promises are faithful*
*and His return, forthcoming,*
*and He guides our sword's every parry and slice.*
*may He be the treasure in the field*
*we seek.*
*we will receive it.*

*travel on, Friend.*